This book was originally published in 1932 under the title of STRAIGHT AND CROOKED THINKING, *and is now being published in a revised and extended form, completely rewritten.*

HOW TO THINK STRAIGHT

THE TECHNIQUE OF APPLYING LOGIC
INSTEAD OF EMOTION

Robert H. Thouless

SIMON AND SCHUSTER

NEW YORK · 1947

NOTE

At the suggestion of Dr. E. M. Glaser, I have added at the end of this book a set of tests of reasoning ability so that readers may test their own power of reasoning and their freedom from prejudice. There are two sets of tests, B and C, which are intended to be of equal difficulty. The idea of putting in two tests is that some readers might like to test themselves before and after reading the book. If they find they do better after reading the book, I shall be gratified, but it is necessary to remember that there are several precautions that must be taken to secure adequate scientific evidence that any such improvement is due to reading the book. For those who find these tests too difficult, there is an easier set, A. Even for those who are going to test themselves with the advanced tests B and C, test A may be found useful as preliminary practice.

I am indebted to Dr. Glaser for his suggestion of this improvement to the book and also for his courtesy in allowing me to see his own much more elaborate system of tests.

ROBERT H. THOULESS

Table of Contents

[vii]

TABLE OF CONTENTS

HOW TO
THINK STRAIGHT

CHAPTER ONE

Emotional Meanings

WHEN we use a word in speech and writing, its most obvious purpose is to point to some thing or relation or property. This is the word's "meaning." We see a small four-footed animal on the road and call it a "dog," indicating that it is a member of the class of four-footed animals we call dogs. The word "dog" as we have used it there has a plain, straightforward, "objective" meaning. We have in no way gone beyond the requirements of exact scientific description.

Let us suppose also that one grandparent of the dog was a collie, another was an Irish terrier, another a fox terrier, and the fourth a bulldog. We can express these facts equally scientifically and objectively by saying that he is a dog of mixed breed. Still we have in no way gone beyond the requirements of exact scientific description.

Suppose, however, that we had called that same animal a "mongrel." The matter is more complicated. We have used a word which objectively means the same as "dog of mixed breed," but which also arouses in our hearers an emotional attitude of disapproval toward that particular dog. A word, therefore, can not only indicate an object, but can also suggest an emotional attitude toward it. Such suggestion of an emotional attitude does go beyond exact and scientific discussion because our approvals and disapprovals are individual—they belong to ourselves and not to the objects we approve or disapprove of. An animal which to the mind of its master is a faithful and noble dog of mixed ancestry may be a "mongrel" to his neighbor whose chickens are chased by it.

Similarly, a Negro may be indicated objectively as a "colored man" or he may be indicated with strong emotional disapproval and contempt as a "nigger." The use of the latter word debases any discussion in which it is used below the level of impartial and objective argument.

Once we are on the lookout for this difference between "objective" and "emotional" meanings, we shall notice that words which carry more or less strong suggestions of emotional attitudes are very common and are ordinarily used in the discussion of such controversial questions as those of politics, morals, and religion. This is one reason why such controversies cannot yet be settled.

There is a well-known saying that the word "firm" can be declined as follows: I am *firm,* thou art *obstinate,* he is *pigheaded.* That is a simple illustration of what is meant. "Firm," "obstinate," and "pigheaded" all have the same objective meaning—that is, following one's own course of action and refusing to be influenced by other people's opinions. They have, however, different emotional meanings: "firm"

[4]

has an emotional meaning of strong approval, "obstinate" of mild disapproval, "pigheaded" of strong disapproval.

In much the same way when, during the World War, thoughts were dominated by emotions, the newspapers contrasted the *spirit* of our heroic boys with the *ruthlessness* of the *Huns,* and the *heroism* of our troops with the enemy's *savagery.* Now, with the more objective attitude that has been brought by the lapse of time, we can look back and see that *spirit* and *ruthlessness* are objectively the same thing, only the one word has an emotional meaning of approval, the other of disapproval. We can see, too, that a soldier going forward under shellfire to probable death is doing the same thing whether he is a German or one of our own countrymen, and that to distinguish between them by applying the word *savagery* to the action of the one and *heroism* to that of the other is to distort reality by using words to make an emotional distinction between two actions which are objectively identical.

Such thinking in wartime may do much harm by leading humane people to condone cruelty. When the ordinarily liberal-minded Swinburne wrote a poem during the Boer War on the death of a British officer who had been blamed for the bad condition of the camps in which the Boer women and children were interned, he said:

Nor heed we more than he what liars dare say
Of mercy's holiest duties left undone

[5]

Towards whelps *and* dams *of* murderou*s foes, whom*
     none
Save we had spared or feared to starve and slay.

Whelps and *dams* clearly mean in objective fact *children* and *wives* with the added meaning of the emotional attitude adopted toward the females and young of wild beasts, while *murderous* means no more in objective fact than that our foes killed us when they could (as we also killed them), with the added emotional meaning of an attitude toward them which is our attitude to those who are guilty of murder.

The use of emotionally toned words is not, of course, always to be condemned. They are always harmful when we are trying to think clearly on a disputable point of fact. In poetry, on the other hand, they have a perfectly proper place, because in poetry (as in some kinds of prose) the arousing of suitable emotions is an important part of the purpose for which the words are used.

In *The Eve of St. Agnes,* Keats has written:

Full on this casement shone the wintry moon,
And threw warm gules on Madeline's fair breast.

These are beautiful lines. Let us notice how much of their beauty follows from the proper choice of emotionally colored words and how completely it is lost if these words are replaced by neutral ones. The words with strikingly emotional meanings are *casement, gules, Madeline, fair,* and *breast. Casement* means simply a kind of window with emotional and romantic associations. *Gules* is the heraldic name for

[6]

red, with the suggestion of romance which accompanies all heraldry. *Madeline* is simply a girl's name, but one calling out favorable emotions absent from a relatively plain and straightforward name. *Fair* simply means, in objective fact, that her skin was white or uncolored—a necessary condition for the colors of the window to show—but also *fair* implies warm emotional preference for an uncolored skin rather than one which is yellow, purple, black, or any of the other colors which skin might be. *Breast* has also similar emotional meanings, and the aim of scientific description might have been equally well attained if it had been replaced by such a neutral word as *chest*.

Let us now try the experiment of keeping these two lines in a metrical form, but replacing all the emotionally colored words by neutral ones, while making as few other changes as possible. We may write:

Full on this window shone the wintry moon,
Making red marks on Jane's uncolored chest.

No one will doubt that all of its poetic value has been knocked out of the passage by these changes. Yet the lines still mean the same in external fact; they still have the same objective meaning. It is only the emotional meaning which has been destroyed.

Now if Keats had been writing a scientific description for a textbook on physics instead of a poem, it would have been necessary for him to have used some such coldly objective terms as the ones into which we have just translated his lines. Such emotionally charged phrases as *warm gules* and *fair breast* would only have obscured the facts to which the scientist exactly but unbeautifully refers when he speaks of "the selective transmission of homogeneous light by pigmented glass."

The purpose of the present book is to deal with the kind of problem in which cold and scientific thinking is required. Most of the practical problems of life are of this order. The fact that I shall abuse the use of emotional thinking in connection with such problems as tariffs, social ownership, revolution, and war does not mean that there is no place for emotional thinking. Poetry, romantic prose, and emotional oratory are all of inestimable value, but their place is not where responsible decisions must be made. The common (almost universal) use of emotional words in political thinking is as much out of place as would be a chemical or statistical formula in the middle of a poem. Real democracy will come only when the solution of national and international problems is carried out by scientific methods of thought, purged of all irrelevant emotion. Into the action which follows decision we can put all the emotion which we have refused to allow in our thinking. Let us think calmly and scientifically about war, and then actively oppose it with all the passion of which we are capable.

The growth of the exact thinking of modern science has been very largely the result of its getting rid of all terms suggesting emotional attitudes and using only those which unemotionally indicate objective facts. It was not always so. The old alchemists called gold and silver "noble" metals, and thought that this emotionally colored word indicated something belonging to the metals themselves from which their properties could be deduced. Other metals were called "base." Although these terms have survived as convenient labels for the modern chemist they carry none of their old emotional significance.

In popular biological discussions, on the other hand, such words are still used with their full emotional meaning, as when the "nobility" of man is contrasted with his alleged "base" origin. In this respect, popular biological discussion differs from that of the textbook and the laboratory, in which are used terms almost as devoid of emotional meaning as those of physics or chemistry.

Psychology is still younger in the ranks of the sciences, and the clearing away from it of emotional words has not gone very far. "Passion," "emotion," "sex" are all terms of our science which carry strong emotional meanings, so that it is difficult to discuss a controversial matter in psychology without using words which rouse strong emotions and confuse all issues. A beginning is being made. "Intelligence" was a subject on which it was difficult to think clearly because it carried so much emotional meaning. Now Professor Spearman has replaced it by what he calls "g" (or the "general factor"), which is a conception derived from the statistical analysis of a large collection of figures, and yet which is in its essence all that was really scientific in the old conception of intelligence. Some day a psychological genius will give us X or Z to replace the old emotional conception of sex, and we shall be able to discuss psychoanalysis as objectively as a mathematical physicist can discuss the quantum theory.

When we turn to politics and international questions, we are still further from straight scientific thinking. Such words as "Bolshevik," "Fascist," "reactionary," "revolutionary," "constitutional," "national honor," etc., are all words used in national and international political thinking which carry more of emotional than of any other meaning. So long as such words are the ordinary terms of rival politicians, how can we hope to think straight in national and international affairs? If a chemist doing an experiment depended on such thought processes as a nation uses in selecting its rulers or in deciding on peace or war with other nations, he would blow up his laboratory. This, however, would be a trivial disaster in comparison with what may result from emotional thinking in politics. Better have a hundred chemical laboratories blown up than the whole of civilization!

We must look forward to and try to help on the day when the thinking about political and international affairs will be as unemotional and as scientific as that about the properties of numbers or the atomic weights of elements. The spirit of impartial investigation of facts unswayed by irrelevant emotions has given us great advances in the sciences. Its triumphs will be even greater when it is applied to the most important affairs of life. We look forward to the day when we shall be able to discuss and settle such questions as Tariffs, Public *vs.* Private Ownership, and

[10]

Disarmament Treaties as successfully as physicists have discussed and settled Einstein's theory of relativity.

Let us try to study a few more examples of the use of words with emotional meanings taken from various sources. Accounts of wars are rich sources of such material, so we are not surprised to find in a book on the French Commune the statement that large numbers of the regular troops were *assassinated* during the street fighting by the Communards, while a much larger number of the latter were *summarily executed* by the regulars. In order to reduce this to a statement of objective fact it is clear that the one word "killed" should be used in place both of *assassinated* and *summarily executed*. We have already noticed how such a choice of words with the same objective but opposite emotional meaning can be used to make us feel sympathetic to one and hostile to the other of two sides in warfare. During the Spanish Civil War, the supporters of the Government referred to themselves as the "Loyalists" and called Franco a "Rebel" or an "Insurgent." The supporters of Franco, on the other hand, called themselves "Nationalists" and referred to their opponents as "Reds." During the conflicts between Red and White forces in Russia and in China, our newspapers told us of the *atrocities* of the Bolsheviks and the *wise severity* of the White commanders. Examination of the details (often possible only long afterwards) shows that the objective facts of an *atrocity* and of *wise severity* are much the same, and that they are not the kind of objective facts which will call out an emotion of approval in a humane person.

A similar choice of words will be noticed in political discussion. A fluent and forcible speech delivered by one of our own party is *eloquent,* a similar speech by one of the opposite party is *fanatical;* again two words with the same objective meaning but with the opposite emotional meanings of approval and strong disapproval. The practical proposals of the opposition, moreover, are *panaceas*—a highly emotional word calling out the strongly disapproving emotions which we feel for those quack patent medicines which make extravagant claims. Those who show enthusiasm in support of proposals with which a speaker disagrees are *crackpots;* while those showing similar enthusiasm on his own side are called *sound.* If a politician wishes to attack some new proposal he has a battery of these and other words with emotional meanings at his disposal. He speaks of "this suggested *panacea* supported only by *fanatical crackpots";* and the proposal is at once discredited in the minds of the majority of people, who like to think of themselves as moderate, distrustful of panaceas, and uninfluenced by windy eloquence. Also, we may notice that it has been discredited without the expenditure of any real thought, for of real objective argument there is none —only the manipulation of words calling out emotion.

It is not, however, only in warfare and politics that such words are used in order to influence opinion more easily than can be done by words embodying real thought. Art criticism is also a good source for this kind of material. Ruskin said of Whistler's Nocturnes: "I have heard and seen much of *Cockney impudence* before now, but never expected to hear a *coxcomb* ask two hundred guineas for *flinging a pot of paint in the public's face.*" As in earlier passages, I have italicized the words or phrases with strongly emotional meanings. Stripped of these and reduced to a statement of objective fact, the passage would have to be paraphrased in some such way as follows: "I have heard and seen much of the behavior of Londoners before now, but never expected to hear a painter ask two hundred guineas for painting a picture which seemed to me to have no meaning." Plainly not much is left of Ruskin's criticism after this operation has been performed on it.

As a last example, we may take a part of an attack made by a newspaper on a novel. This runs: "Its *vicious plea* for the acknowledgment and *condonation* of *sexual perversity*, and the grounds on which it is based, loosen the very *sheet anchor of conduct.*" This passage calls out such strong emotions of abhorrence that most readers will be content to condemn the novel without further inquiry. Yet the effect is gained entirely by the choice of words with emotional meanings. It happens to deal with a subject on which emotions are strong, so a dispassionate examination is all the more necessary. We note that a *plea* is simply an argument, plus a suggestion of repugnance for the kind of argument used; that *condonation* is tolerance plus an emotional suggestion that such toleration is indefensible; that *sexual* means

[13]

something in the life of love of which we disapprove, and that a *perversity* is an unusualness plus an emotional suggestion of abhorrence. The loosening of a *sheet anchor* is a metaphor implying change and suggesting to a landsman the emotion of fear, while *conduct* is simply behavior of which we approve.

So reduced to its bare bones of statement of objective fact (ignoring for a moment the special difficulties raised by the word *vicious*), the passage becomes: "Its argument for the acknowledgment and tolerance of unusualness in the life of love, and the grounds on which it is based, change the principles of behavior." This clearly is an important statement if it is true, but is not enough in itself to condemn the book, because undoubtedly our principles of behavior do need changing from time to time. We can only decide intelligently whether or not they need changing in the particular case under discussion, when we have made a dispassionate statement of what the proposed changes are and why they are defended. As in all other cases, discussion of the question with emotionally charged words obscures the problem and makes a sensible decision difficult or impossible.

The word *vicious* has some special difficulties of its own. It arouses emotions of disapproval, but there is no word with the same objective meaning which would not. If we call the book bad, corrupt, or evil, the same emotions would be aroused. So we cannot perform the simple operation of replacing *vicious* by an emotionally neutral word with the same objective meaning. Can we then leave it out altogether, on the ground that it has no objective meaning, but that it is used merely to arouse emotion?

Here we are up against a problem about which there has been much dispute. Some people consider that all such words as "good," "bad," "beautiful," "ugly," only indicate one's own emotional reactions toward actions or things and in no sense properties of the actions or things themselves. But when we see a man steal a penny from a child and we call his action "bad," we are in fact saying something meaningful about the action itself and not merely about our own feelings. As to what that something is we may leave the philosophers to dispute; it may only be that the man's action has subtracted from the total amount of human happiness. So to say a book is *vicious* is not the same kind of thing as contrasting the *slaughter* of regular troops by Communards with the *execution* of the Communards by regular soldiers. The statement that the book is *vicious* has a meaning which is not merely emotional, although, of course, the statement may not be true.

On the other hand, it is clearly not quite the same kind of meaning as a simple statement of outside fact such as "This is a book." Whether the book is good or bad is a real question, but it is a question peculiarly difficult to decide. Our own statement one way or the other is likely to be nothing but a reflection of our own personal prejudices and to have, therefore, no sort of scientific exactness. At the same time, such words certainly arouse strong emotions and should, therefore, be used sparingly in honest argument. The

[15]

use of words implying moral judgments in the course of argument is very generally an attempt to distort the hearers' view of the truth by arousing emotions.

If we are trying to decide a simple question of fact, such words should be left out, because it is easier to settle one question at a time. If a man is accused of poisoning his wife, the prosecuting attorney should not say, "This *scoundrel* who hounded his wife to her grave." The question to be decided is whether the man did poison his wife. If he did, he is a "scoundrel" undoubtedly, but calling him a scoundrel does not help to decide the question of fact. On the contrary, it makes a correct decision more difficult by rousing emotions of hatred for the accused in the minds of the jury. Another obvious objection to the use of the word "scoundrel" before the man is convicted, which puts it in the ranks of "crooked thinking," is that it "begs the question" or assumes what is to be proved. The man is only a scoundrel if he is guilty, and yet the word has been used in the course of an argument to prove that he is guilty.

These two objections can be urged against the word "vicious" in the condemnation of a book quoted above. It calls up strong emotions making a just decision of the nature of the book difficult, and it assumes exactly what the article professes to prove— that the book is a bad one.

The aim of this chapter has been to distinguish one kind of crooked thinking, in the hope that those who recognize how their opinions can be twisted away from the truth by the use of words with emotional meanings may be able to recognize this source of error and to guard themselves against it. Those of its readers who have found anything new to them in the ideas of this chapter should not, I suggest, be content simply to read the chapter, but should try to do some practical work on its subject matter. If you were studying botany, you would not be content merely to read books on botany. If you were, that would not carry you far in botanical knowledge. Instead you would gather plants from the hedges and weeds from your garden, dissecting them, examining them with a microscope or magnifying glass, and drawing them in your notebook. Psychology too should be studied by practical methods. Emotional thinking (like most of the other kinds of crooked thinking we shall be studying) is as common as a weed. It is to be found in the leading articles of newspapers, in the words of people carrying on discussions on political, religious, or moral questions, and in the speeches made by public men when these deal with controversial matters. In order to understand it, we should collect specimens by putting them down on paper and then we should dissect them. Current political and social controversy in the United States abounds in such words and phrases as "crackpots," "economic royalists," "the abundant life," "bureaucracy"—or, on the street level —"scabs," "finks," "nigger-lovers." The *New York Herald Tribune* habitually referred to the child labor bill for New York State as the "youth control bill"; the Hearst press dubbed the New Deal the "Raw Deal"; Communists use the words "Trotzkyite" and

[17]

"Fascist" to cover a multitude of sinners; Secretary Ickes managed to get some powerful emotional undertones from Ferdinand Lundberg's phrase, "America's Sixty Families."

With these ideas and phrases in mind, it is not difficult to set forth on a practical search for truth. I suggest that readers should copy out controversial phrases from newspapers, books, or speeches which contain emotionally colored words. Then they should underline all the emotional words, afterwards rewriting the passages with the emotional words replaced by neutral ones. Examine the passage then in its new form in which it merely states objective facts without indicating the writer's emotional attitude toward them, and see whether it is still good evidence for the proposition it is trying to prove. If it is, the passage is a piece of straight thinking in which emotionally colored words have been introduced merely as an ornament. If not, it is crooked thinking, because the conclusion depends not on the objective meaning of the passage but on the emotions roused by the words.

When we condemn such a use of emotional words in writings and speeches, we must remember that this is a symptom of a more deep-seated evil—their prevalence in our own private, unexpressed thinking. Many of our highly colored political speakers whose speeches stir us as we are stirred by romantic poetry show themselves unable to think calmly and objectively on any subject. They have so accustomed themselves to think in emotionally toned words that they can no longer think in any other way. They should have been poets or professional orators, but certainly not statesmen.

It really does not matter much if we sometimes use emotional words. We all do when we are trying to produce conviction. What does matter is that we should not lose the power to think without them. So a more important exercise than any we can perform on written material is one we can perform on our own minds. When we catch ourselves thinking in emotional phraseology, let us form a habit of translating our thoughts into emotionally neutral words. So we can guard ourselves from ever being so enslaved by emotional words and phrases that they prevent us from thinking objectively when we need to do so—that is, whenever we have to come to a decision on any debatable matter.

In the same way, I suggest that those who wish to learn more of the nature of crooked thinking should, after the reading of each of the later chapters, try to collect specimens of the tricks described from the sources I have mentioned. In some cases I shall suggest practical operations which can be carried out on them in order to make clear the nature of the crooked thinking (as, for example, in Chapter Six the provision of a new setting for doubtful propositions which run along the lines of our own thought habits). These operations should be carried out on the material you have collected. In this way it will be possible to gain a better mastery of the subject and a better protection against your own intellectual exploitation by unscrupulous speakers than by merely reading books.

[19]

CHAPTER TWO

All and Some

Dᴜʀɪɴɢ the 1936 Presidential election, the Republican Party represented this line of argument to the voters: "If Liberty is lost, Tyranny reigns: Vote Republican." The first part of the statement is an argument. As often happens in practice, a great part of the argument is left out, but we can easily supply the missing part, and the result is an argument which, at first sight, looks like a correct one. It runs like this: (1) A condition in which liberty is lost is one in which tyranny reigns. (2) The New Deal establishes conditions in which liberty is lost. (3) Therefore, the New Deal is a condition in which tyranny reigns.

Now, this has the general form of a correct argument, and the statements (1) and (2) are both correct, so the conclusion must also be correct, provided that identical terms in (1) and (2) have identical meanings. This important provision is not fulfilled, however, so the conclusion is not proved. Moreover, whatever may be our views on the New Deal, we see that the conclusion is wrong in fact.

The fallacy lies in the omission of the word "all" or "some" in front of "liberty." Statement (1) is only true if "all" is the missing word, while (2) is only true if "some" is the missing word. The fallacy is quite clear in the extended form of the argument, but it is concealed in its original shortened form, "If liberty is lost, tyranny reigns." It is true that under the New Deal some liberty is lost—the liberty to sell stocks short, for example. But the argument suggests, quite untruly, that under the New Deal all liberty is lost, for it is only when all liberty is lost that tyranny can be said to reign.

We can put this in a more general way by saying that a common form of dishonest argument is the statement "A is B" when "some A is B" would be true, but in which the untrue statement "all A is B" is implied for the rest of the argument. The world of propaganda and argumentation is full of such statements. Our fathers refused to allow women to vote because "women are politically incapable." Undoubtedly some women are incapable of making sensible political decisions (as are some men), but certainly not all. As we have seen, Swinburne condoned the bad conditions of the camps in which Boer women and children were interned during the South African war because our foes were "murderous." Yet he could not reasonably have maintained more than that "some" were murderous, while his plea was only reasonable if "all" were murderous. Massacres of Jews in the Middle Ages, of aristocrats in the French Revolution, of communists and anticommunists in countries of our own time which are more bloodthirsty in their politics than we are—these are all examples of the

[21]

readiness of men to act on the proposition that "all A's are evil" when A stands for men of another nation, race, or creed. Yet it is apparent to the impartial observer that the truth is merely that "some A's are evil" (as equally are some not-A's). Cruelty and injustice are resulting now, as they have throughout the history of the world, from this piece of crooked thinking.

I do not, of course, wish to go so far as to say that all general statements of the form "all A is B" must necessarily be false. That itself would be a general statement that is certainly false. I only wish to suggest the more moderate position that a great many are. Also that their falsity is often concealed by leaving out the word "all," so that, if challenged, they can slink past as if "some A is B" were meant although they are used in argument as if "all A is B" were true.

One reason why we are so much inclined to say or to imply "all" in a sentence which would be true with the word "some" is that a sentence with "some" says so little. Suppose that we say quite truthfully: "Some red-haired people are bad-tempered." We have said so little that it was hardly worth saying at all, for so also are some people bad-tempered who are not red-haired, and some people are certainly not bad-tempered who are red-haired. So we have not said much when we have merely said: "Some red-haired people are bad-tempered"; not enough for it to be worth while for a red-haired person to argue against the proposition.

Surely there must be a way of saying something

about the connection between bad temper and red hair which (whether true or not) would have meant more than the simple statement with "some," and which would yet not be the obviously untrue statement with "all."

There is, in fact, such a form of statement, and it is one which is very commonly found in some of the newer sciences. Particularly commonly is it to be found in the sciences of psychology, economics, and sociology, which deal with such very variable things as human beings about whom very few true statements can be made containing the word "all." It is one of the reasons for much crooked thinking that the kind of statement we require is not found in common speech. Yet it is a very necessary form of statement even for everyday thinking.

The form of statement we need is this: "Red-haired people tend to be (or have a tendency to be) bad-tempered." This does not mean that all red-haired people are bad-tempered or that all people not red-haired are good-tempered or even that there are a greater number of bad-tempered, red-haired people than of bad-tempered people without red hair, but simply that there is a larger proportion of bad-tempered people among the red-haired, that is, that (other things being equal) a person with red hair is more likely to be bad-tempered than a person without red hair.

Let us suppose that we studied a random sample of a thousand people—a large enough group to be taken as a fair sample of the population as a whole. Let us

[23]

suppose that we divided these into a group of two hundred who had red hair and eight hundred who had not. Then let us suppose that we divided each of these groups into those who were and those who were not bad-tempered, and found fifty bad-tempered people among the red-haired and a hundred among the not red-haired. We have now divided our thousand people into four classes, and every one of the thousand must fall into one or other of these classes. The result is summarized in the diagram below.

50 BAD-TEMPERED RED-HAIRED	150 not bad-tempered RED-HAIRED
100 BAD-TEMPERED not red-haired	700 not bad-tempered not red-haired

Now these figures contain a complete answer to our question: Do red-haired people tend to be bad-tempered? Let us examine them carefully and see what they mean. There are twice as many bad-tempered people among the not red-haired as among the red-haired. But this does not mean that red-haired people are less likely to be bad-tempered than others because there is a smaller total number of the red-haired. In fact, one quarter of the red-haired are bad-tempered and only one eighth of the others. So the answer to our question is obviously "Yes." A bookmaker could safely give you odds of about seven to one against a particular person without red hair being bad-tempered, but he could only offer you about three to one against a particular red-haired person being bad-tempered. The chance of a red-haired person being bad-tempered will be just double the chance of a not red-haired person being bad-tempered.

The several different ways in which we can express that relationship between these figures make it possible to conclude that red-hairedness tends to be accompanied by bad temper. Perhaps the best of them is this: If the proportion of bad-tempered people among the red-haired is greater than the proportion of bad-tempered people among the population as a whole, this means that redness of hair tends to be accompanied by badness of temper. In the figures we have taken, for example, the proportion of bad-tempered people among the red-haired is 50 in 200, *i.e.* one fourth, while the proportion among our group as a whole (red-haired and non-red-haired lumped together) is only 150 to 1000 or three twentieths. Now one fourth is five twentieths, so there is clearly a larger proportion of bad-tempered among the red-haired than among the group as a whole (nearly twice as great). So if these figures were correct it would be proved that redness of hair tends to be accompanied by bad temper.

The method of proof I have given is one which will be familiar to many of my readers as the statistical method of association. It is necessary to mention that I have given only the elementary part of it and that there are complications which must be considered in practice. If, for example, our figures seemed to show only a small association between red hair and bad temper, it would be necessary to discover whether this could reasonably be attributed to chance or whether, on the other hand, it indicated a real association between the two characters. A further complication arises from the influence of "partial associations." For example, if more women than men had red hair and more women than men had bad temper, then figures drawn from a mixed group of women and men might seem to indicate an association between red hair and bad temper, although figures drawn only from a group of men or only from a group of women showed that red hair and bad temper were entirely independent of one another. A full discussion of these complications will be found in any textbook on statistical methods.

We have spent rather a long time in detailed examination of a trivial example of no practical importance. That was simply because I wanted to make as clear as possible the principles involved, without complicating the matter by bringing in questions about which my readers felt strongly. Obviously, however, exactly the same line of thought applies to many controversial questions of the highest practical importance. We see easily how absurd it would be if two men set themselves to argue on the question of whether red-haired people were bad-tempered, and one of them said they were and "proved" it merely by pointing to members of the red-haired, bad-tempered class and of the non-red-haired, non-bad-tempered class, while his opponent similarly "proved" his case that red-haired people were not bad-tempered by pointing to the members of the non-bad-tempered, red-haired class and the bad-tempered, non-red-haired class. It would be about as easy for the second man as for the first, because in our group of a thousand he would have one hundred of the one class and a hundred and fifty of the other to point to. Yet it is as clear as it can be that neither of these two men would be proving his case at all, and also that the case could not be proved by the kind of argument they are using —a kind of argument we may call "proof by selected instances."

There are, of course, innumerable examples of statements of the same order as the ones we have discussed. As a result of the Moscow treason trials, it is commonly said that Russians are cruel and murderous people. This can hardly mean that all Russians are cruel and murderous. What is really meant must be that there is a larger proportion of cruel and murderous people among the Russians than among the world as a whole, *i.e.*, that Russians tended to be cruel and murderous. How much real evidence is there for supposing this to be true rather than the contrary proposition that as large a proportion of good and kindly people are to be found in Russia as anywhere else?

This is clearly a question on which none of us can bring forward the numerical evidence which would alone constitute sound proof. There are other questions on which the required numerical evidence is

[27]

available, but which are nevertheless argued by the crude and inaccurate method of selected instances. We may take as an example the problem of whether capital punishment is an effective preventative of murder. Upholders of capital punishment can point to countries which have no capital punishment and a large number of murders, and those which have capital punishment and a small number of murders. Their opponents can point to countries with no capital punishment and few murders and to others with capital punishment and many murders. This is merely proof by selected instances and carries us no farther. The real proof must be an examination of the numerical relationships of all of these four classes of countries as shown above.

Lastly, let us consider the question of whether co-operative enterprise is more or less efficient than private enterprise. This is undoubtedly a practical question of great importance. Yet we find speeches, articles, and whole books of those defending private enterprise simply made up of a selection of unsuccessful co-operative enterprises (such as the Belgian State railways) and of successful private ones (such as Ford's motor factories). Their opponents similarly retort by a selection of successful co-operative enterprises (as those in the Scandinavian countries) and unsuccessful private ones (of which the United States has offered many examples since 1929). This is, again, argument by selected instances and is as incapable of settling this problem as it is of settling any other.

Do not suppose that I am suggesting that on such subjects as these we must have no opinions at all. On the contrary, all the controversies I have mentioned (with the exception of that of the association between red hair and bad temper) are ones on which I have strong opinions myself. On practical questions of urgent importance we must make up our minds one way or the other even when we know that the evidence is incomplete. To refuse to make up our minds is equivalent to deciding to leave things as they are (which is just as likely as any other to be the wrong solution).

But the fact that we must make up our minds in practice is no reason for failing to think straight on such questions by mistaking incomplete for complete evidence. We must not suppose that our case can be proved by merely selecting instances favorable to our view while we ignore other instances. Nor must we think that our case is disproved when our opponents similarly select instances favorable to themselves. Always we must be on the lookout for the real proof— the statistical proof, for example, as to whether co-operative enterprise tends or does not tend to be accompanied by increased efficiency. We must remember also that such proof can only come from the impartial researches of experts and not by any thinking or argumentation we can do for ourselves.

In the day to which we look forward when the running of national and international affairs becomes an exact science, the political expenditure which now goes to paying orators and subsidizing newspapers will be spent in paying for such research as this. But that day seems still far ahead.

In the meantime, we have to make up our minds on such evidence as is available, and that, we know, is incomplete. This means that although we must make up our minds definitely we must not do so finally, but we must be willing to be guided by experience, being sure that experience will often lead us to change our minds on subjects about which we have felt most certain.

CHAPTER THREE

Some Dishonest Tricks in Argument

W E have already noticed that a statement of the form "all A is B" is very rarely true and is very easily disproved. It is easily disproved for the obvious reason that a single instance of an A that is not B is sufficient to overthrow it. If, for example, a man maintains that all pacifists are cowards, his opponent need point to only one pacifist who has shown courage by facing death bravely and his opponent's case is overthrown. If, on the other hand, his opponent had maintained the more moderate proposition that some pacifists are cowards, he could not have been defeated, for he could undoubtedly have brought forward one or more examples of pacifists who were cowards and his contention would then be established.

This suggests that, in an argument, a man who maintains an extreme position (such as "all A is B") is in a very unfavorable position for successful controversy. Many people consciously or unconsciously adopt a trick based on this principle. This is the trick of driving their opponents to defend a more extreme position than is really necessary for their purpose. Against an incautious opponent this can often be done simply by contradicting his more moderate assertions until in the heat of controversy he boldly puts forward more and more extreme ones.

Let us suppose, for example, that two men are arguing about the condition of Russia under the Communist Government. M. maintains that the people are starving, that industry is totally disorganized, and that the workers are only kept from a successful counterrevolution by terror. N. holds against him the more moderate position that things are not as bad as M. paints them, and that in some respects the workers are better off than they were before the revolution. Clearly M. is holding a position less easy to defend than the other, and we should expect the victory to go to N. So it probably would if N. were content to stick to the very moderate set of propositions that he has laid down, which are really all that is needed to overthrow M. As the argument goes on, however, M. makes exaggerated statements of the bad conditions of the workers in Russia, and by a natural reaction N. makes equally wild statements of their prosperity, until he is maintaining a picture of universal well-being in Russia which his facts are quite insufficient to support. M. now assumes the offensive and brings forward facts sufficient to overthrow the extremely favorable view of internal conditions in Russia which N. has been incautious enough to defend, and N. loses the argument. Yet he had a winning case to begin with. How often we see an adventurous controversialist wrecked in this way.

A person cautious in argument will not, however, be so easily led to court defeat. He will constantly reaffirm the moderate and defensible position with which he started, and the extreme statements of his opponent will be rebutted by evidence instead of leading him on to equally extreme statements on the other side. Against such a person, however, a similar trick is used very commonly in a more blatantly dishonest way. He has asserted moderately and truly that "some A is B," but his opponent argues against the proposition that "all A is B." If he answers his opponent's arguments at all, he can only do so by defending the proposition "all A is B." Then he has fallen into the trap. If he avoids this by reasserting his original position, his opponent often brings against him a particularly meaningless piece of sophistry which runs: "But you ought logically to say that all A is B if you think some A is B."

A public speaker, for example, maintained that a country with as much distress as there is in England at the present time could not afford heavy expenditure on the expensive luxuries of the rich. This was a moderate and reasonable proposition. One of his hearers accused him afterwards of inconsistency in attacking all expenditure on what were not necessities, since, presumably, the speaker had recreations of his own on which he expended money.

The speaker refused to have his proposition extended and reasserted his original statement that not all expenditure on recreation was undesirable, but that excessive expenditure was, pointing out that he had already shown that this was his view by arguing that some amount of luxury expenditure of this kind was desirable for everybody. His opponent now said: "To be logically consistent, you ought to disapprove of all luxury expenditure if you disapprove of expenditure on grouse moors and deer forests." To this unreasonable assertion I know of no satisfactory reply except to deny that there is any such logical necessity. The statement that "some A is B" is as logically adequate as "all A is B," and is, in fact, more likely to be true.

Let us call this device the "extension" of one's opponent's proposition. It can be done either by luring him on to extend it himself in the heat of argument or, more impudently, by misrepresenting what he said. It is a very common trick, often done involuntarily. The remedy is always to refuse to accept any extension, but to reaffirm what one originally said.

Other ways in which this trick may be used will occur to my readers. An example of a more disguised form of it is: "You suppose that this piece of social reform will bring in the millennium." The person attacked must reply: "I don't suppose that it will bring in the millennium, or even that in itself it will solve all our more immediate problems. I only maintain that it will do something to reduce poverty by producing a more just distribution of wealth." Clearly, if this is true, it is all that the speaker need maintain in order to convince his hearers that the reform is a desirable one. If he were led to make further claims, he would have fallen into the trap of the "extension," and would find his proposition more difficult to defend. If he were foolish enough to walk so far into the trap as to maintain that his reform would bring about a perfect social order (implied by the word "millennium"), his proposition would become impossible to defend.

Let us return to the attempt to force an extension by saying to one's opponent, "Logically, you ought to believe that all A is B" (that is, to maintain the extended proposition). This is a sample of a trick which perhaps deserves separate notice—that of using a sophistical formula in order to try to force a victory in argument. This particular one is fairly common. When, in a university, one party wished to admit women to its degrees with certain restrictions, their opponents who did not want to give them degrees at all urged that to be logically consistent they should either give women no degrees or give them on the same conditions as they did to men.

This can be a sound argument and not a dishonest trick on one condition—that the proposers of the moderate proposition are defending it by reasons which would equally apply to the extended proposition (if, for example, the supporters of women's degrees had given reasons for their restrictions which would have been equally good reasons for not giving degrees to women at all). In fact, they did not; their reasons (whether good or bad) were reasons for restriction and not for refusal.

Another sophistical formula which we shall commonly meet is never an honest argument. When a man maintains an extreme position, as, for example, that all Negroes are incapable of intellectual development, he can be quite properly refuted by his opponent pointing to Booker T. Washington, Paul Robeson, President Borno, and other intellectually distinguished Negroes. He may then try to escape by saying: "These are exceptions that prove the rule."

The attempt to ignore a sound refutation of an extreme position by the use of this formula, "the exception proves the rule," is a fairly common trick and is obviously a dishonest one. It can be dealt with by pointing out (what is obvious) that an exception does not prove that a general rule is true, but that it is false. One can also assert that "prove" in this passage originally had the meaning "test." If one is anxious to discover the truth and not to triumph over one's opponent, one may try to discover what more moderate proposition is true. This may be, for example, that the average intellectual achievement of Negroes is (whether from lack of opportunity or from inborn difference of average intelligence) less than that of whites.

Another common trick in controversy may be called the "diversion." This is the defense of a proposition by another proposition which does not prove the first one, but which diverts the discussion to another question, generally one on which the person who makes the diversion feels more certain. I was, for example, once staying with a man who told me indignantly that he had heard a sermon in which the preacher had said that in Russia the workingman was esteemed more highly than in any other country. Although I had no more exact knowledge of the truth about conditions in Russia than most of my fellow countrymen, I felt

[36]

that of the things which might be said in favor of Russia this was one of the most probable, so I said cautiously: "Well, that is quite likely to be true, isn't it?" "True!" my host exclaimed, "it's a pack of lies. Do you know that during the last few years in Russia, over twenty thousand people have been killed simply because they were Christians?"

This is a clear diversion, for my host would not seriously have maintained the proposition that a country in which Christians are killed cannot be a country in which workingmen are held in high esteem. They are two different statements. Either or both may be true or false, but the truth of one does not imply the falsity of the other.

Diversions occur very commonly in arguments. In the example I have quoted the diversion was not made deliberately. Sometimes, however, it is. A good source from which to study the successful use of the diversion is to be found in the correspondence columns of our newspapers. Nearly every controversy that is started is not carried to a conclusion because one side or the other creates a diversion in the third or fourth letter. A discussion of the rights and wrongs of the Civil War may, for example, in the course of half a dozen letters, change into an acrimonious squabble as to the religious opinions of President Lincoln. More commonly it degenerates into a discussion as to which of the two disputants is the more reliable historian, or shows the greater respect for "logic." Indeed diversions from any argument to a discussion of the personal characteristics of the disputants are so common as probably to form much the greater number of diversions. Most of the disputes of the streets seem to end in this way even when they begin with a relatively objective problem (such, for example, as which of two motorcars was on the wrong side of the road).

Into the class of diversions we must put, too, the trick of fastening on a trivial point in an opponent's argument, defeating him on that, and then leaving it to be supposed that he has been defeated on the main question. A man bringing forward a large number of facts in support of a contention may very well bring forward one, at least, that is not correct. The incorrectness of that fact may not be enough to undermine his conclusion, but an opponent who fastens on that one fact and proves its wrongness can easily create the impression that the whole position of the other is discredited although, in fact, it is untouched. He has gained a victory by a diversion although the diversion has not been, as in our earlier examples, to a new question, but to a side issue in the question under discussion.

A more impudent form of the same trick is the use of an "irrelevant objection." This is a denial of a fact brought forward (perhaps in illustration) by a disputant, when the truth of this fact is of no importance at all (and not merely of minor importance) to the main argument. In a dispute I heard recently between two philosophers, one wanted to illustrate his argument by reference to a rectangle. So he looked round the room and pointed to a rectangular panel on the wall. His opponent objected that this could not be taken as an example because sufficiently careful measurement would show that its sides were not exactly straight and its angles not exactly right angles. This was clearly a diversion by irrelevant objection, since the argument of the first speaker was quite unaffected by the properties of the particular rectangle he took as his example.

The diversion by irrelevant objection sounds as if it were a trick too clumsy and too obvious to be successfully employed. In fact, it is often very successful, particularly when the objection is of a humorous character. This is not because the nature of the device is not obvious, but because the person against whom it is used is in danger of appearing somewhat ridiculous in his efforts to bring the discussion back to the point from which it is diverted. The audience is more willing to laugh with the person who made the diversion than to follow the laborious efforts of his opponent to return to seriousness. It is a mean way of obtaining a reputation for being clever, and the person who habitually makes humorous diversions in a serious argument deserves no sympathy. The trick is widespread and is as often a vice of senators and judges as it is of superficial debaters in less dignified surroundings.

The diversion can, of course, be used by the defender of a proposition as well as by the person who attacks it. When a man has made a statement and finds himself hard pressed in its defense, he may divert the discussion in a direction more in his favor by substituting for the original statement one that sounds like it but which is easier to defend. Some people habitually begin a discussion by stating an extreme proposition and then, when this is attacked, they substitute for it a more moderate statement. They thus gain a double advantage. By the original statement they challenge attention and gain an undeserved reputation for being bold thinkers, while the later diversion enables them to escape the crushing defeat in argument which they would otherwise suffer. It is easy for the onlookers to be led to suppose that the original extreme statement is the one that has been successfully defended.

The remedy for all cases of diversion is to bring the discussion back to the question from which it started. This is not, in practice, always an easy thing to do, since an unscrupulous debater will then object that you are evading his arguments. With care and good temper, however, it can generally be done.

There is a device related to diversion which we may mention here. That is the trick of bringing in defense of a statement another statement which does not in fact prove it, trusting that one's opponent will not challenge the proof. This can often be insured by making the supporting statement a reference to a learned theory of which one's opponent will be afraid to confess his ignorance, or, at any rate, making the supporting statement in a matter so obscure that one's opponent fears that it would show shameful ignorance if he confessed that he did not see the connection.

Opponents of democratic government, for instance, frequently declare that the doctrine proclaiming men to be born "free and equal" contradicts "human nature." In like manner, those who oppose raising wages declare that a more equal distribution of wealth would remove all initiative and reduce the living standard to a universally degraded level. Let us call this method that of the "inconsequent argument." The form of the inconsequent argument is simply "A must be true because of B," when, in fact, A does not follow from B at all. Its deliberate use would imply shameless dishonesty and is, I think, rare. Carelessness and the idleness which leads men not to examine the steps not actually stated in their arguments make the inconsequent argument a fairly common one. The remedy is to ask your opponent to make clear how B is supposed to prove A. This is to admit ignorance, and if the argument is not really inconsequent and your opponent can clearly show the connection, he will gain an advantage. If not, however, your confession of ignorance has done you no harm. Too much fear of admitting ignorance lays you open to much crookedness in argument.

The inconsequent argument is related to the diversion because, in each case, as proof of a proposition a statement is offered which does not, in fact, prove it. They differ in the later direction of the argument. If it goes off on to a discussion of the new proposition, a diversion has been made; if the new proposition is brought forward not to be discussed itself but to settle the discussion on the original point, we have an inconsequent argument. In the example given above of an attempted diversion from the position of

[41]

working men in Russia to the persecution of Christians, the new proposition is so simple itself that a diversion to it is likely to be the course of any further argument which may take place. If my opponent had referred to some obscure theory of Marx or to an official report I had not read, then, if his argument still did not prove his contention, it would have been an inconsequent argument. It could not have made a diversion because I should not have had the knowledge necessary to discuss his new point. It must, on the contrary, have settled in his favor the original proposition, unless I had been willing to confess my ignorance of the alleged proof he was bringing forward.

Another common trick of argument which I have never seen recorded but which appears to be worth exposing is that of presenting the view which is to be accepted as the mean between two extremes. We all love a compromise, and when someone recommends a position to us as an intermediate one between two extreme positions, we feel a strong tendency to accept it. Knowing this, people of the most diverse opinions present their views to us in this way.

During the American presidential elections of 1936 the Republican, Democratic, Socialist, and Communist Parties all resorted to this device, and all represented themselves as advocating a moderate course between two extremes. The Republicans represented Roosevelt as an extreme and irresponsible radical who was attempting to establish a personal bureaucratic dictatorship. They admitted that mistakes had been

[42]

made during the 1920's and that some government regulation had become necessary as a result of changing conditions. Their program, they said, embodied a wise compromise between individualism and government interference.

The Democrats, on the other hand, represented the Republicans as extreme reactionaries, Bourbons, and "economic royalists" who would revert to the discredited "rugged individualism" of the Hoover era. They pointed to the rise of Communism and Fascism in Europe and proclaimed that their program offered the only middle course between the extremes of untrammeled individualism and ruthless dictatorship. Meanwhile the Socialists called down a plague upon both the Democrats and Republicans who were represented as being as much alike as Tweedledum and Tweedledee since both parties had the same underlying aim: the preservation of capitalism. According to the Socialist theory, the only choice that confronted the American people was whether the change from capitalism to socialism should be made gradually and peacefully or suddenly and violently. The Socialists represented themselves as the advocates of evolution as distinguished from the Communist who in the past had advocated revolution. In other words, it was the Socialist Party, not the Democrats or Republicans, that was offering the only real golden mean.

It remained for the Communists—hitherto associated with extreme revolutionary measures—to take the most ingenious line of all. To begin with, they dropped their radicalism and represented the election as a kind of popular referendum on the issue of Fascism. Roosevelt, they said, embodied the moderate, progressive, democratic forces. He did not go far enough for their taste, but he was infinitely preferable to Landon, the pseudo-Fascist. For their part they offered to co-operate loyally with any group sincerely devoted to democracy and progressive principles—with one exception—the followers of Leon Trotzky. Furthermore, the followers of Trotzky had joined the Socialist Party and had thus identified that group—rather than the Communists—with those irresponsible, extreme, impractical tactics that have made all revolutionaries suspect in moderate circles.

The average American, subjected to these arguments, had every reason to arrive at rather melancholy conclusions about the golden mean. Clearly, the truth does not always lie in the mean position between two extremes, and however attractive such a notion may be it is of no practical use in discovering where the truth lies, because every view can be represented as the mean between two extremes.

A second reason for distrusting this piece of crooked thinking is the fact that when we have two extreme positions and a middle one between them, the truth is just as likely to lie on one extreme as in the middle position. If I wished to convince you that two and two make five, I might commend it to you as the safe middle position between the exaggerations on the one hand of the extremists, who assert that two and two make four, and on the other of those who assert the equally extreme position that two and two make six. I should appeal to you as moderate men and women not to be led away by either of these extreme parties, but to follow with me the safe middle path of asserting that two and two make five. As moderate men and women, perhaps you would believe me, but you and I would alike be wrong because the truth would lie with one party of the extremists.

It is not, of course, to be supposed that every representation of a position as a mean between two extremes is necessarily a dishonest argument. It may not be an argument at all. It is a teaching device which I use frequently myself and, I think, quite honestly. When, for example, I want to explain how much of decent and socialized behavior in human beings is based on instinct, I contrast Hobbes' idea that men are naturally in a state of war with one another, and are only kept good citizens by fear, with that of Kropotkin, who supposed that instinctively we were entirely altruistic and only became self-seeking through the bad effects of the social institutions under which we live in a capitalist society. I point out the objections to both of these views and then develop a middle view that there are both instinctive social tendencies and instinctive antisocial tendencies. I do not say or suggest that this view is true because it is a mean between the views of Hobbes and Kropotkin; I have only used these views as a help to making clear what my position is. Any view can conveniently be explained by comparing it with other views, and it can best be explained by comparing it with two sets of views differing from it in opposite directions. It is, however, dangerously easy to slip from this honest use of comparison to the crooked thinking of suggesting that a position ought to be accepted because it is the mean between two extremes.

This is a trick so commonly used that many people do not recognize it as crooked thinking at all. It cannot, therefore, be dealt with effectively simply by pointing out that the trick is being used. It can, I think, best be rebutted by pointing out that other positions which would not be accepted by one's opponent (as, for example, the position one happens to be defending) can also be represented as mean positions between two extremes.

CHAPTER FOUR

Some Logical Fallacies

THE trick of suggesting that a proposition ought to be believed because it can be expressed as a mean between two extremes is generally used in an open and undisguised form. There are other faults in reasoning which would be obvious to the most inefficient reasoner if they were displayed in a simple manner, but which may well be overlooked in the actual course of argument where many of the steps are left out. An exhaustive account of the kind of deductions which cannot lead to a valid conclusion may be found in any textbook on logic. Here we shall be content to describe one example which is not uncommon in practice—the syllogism with an undistributed middle term.

One of the most familiar forms of deduction analyzed by the traditional logic runs as follows:

> *All mammals are animals,*
> *All cats are mammals,*
> *Therefore, all cats are animals.*

Translated into general terms, this becomes:

> *All A is B,*
> *All C is A,*
> *Therefore, all C is B.*

[47]

The argument is known as the syllogism in the mood of *Barbara*. One does not need the intelligence of an Einstein to see that if the first two of these statements (the premises) are correct, then the third (the conclusion) rigidly follows. The matter can be made even clearer by the use of a diagram.

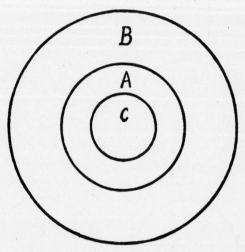

If B, A, and C are represented by the areas of the large, the medium, and the small circles respectively, it is clear that the conditions that A falls entirely inside B and that C falls entirely inside A necessarily imply that C falls entirely inside B.

Now let us turn to a closely similar form of argument from which no conclusion follows.

> *All dogs are mammals,*
> *All cats are mammals,*
> *Therefore, all cats are dogs.*

[48]

In general terms this is:

> *All A is B,*
> *All C is B,*
> *Therefore, all C is A.*

Clearly, the conclusion does not follow, for the premises are consistent with what is represented by any one of the four diagrams below.

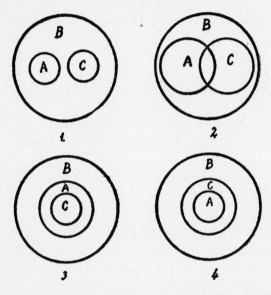

All are alike in showing both A and C as totally inclosed in B (all cats and all dogs are mammals). This, of course, is all that is stated in the premises. The different arrangements of the inner circles show all the conclusions as to the relationship between dogs and cats which are consistent with these premises. The relationship indicated by diagram No. 1, in which no cats are also dogs, happens to be true in fact. That of the second diagram, however, in which some cats are dogs, while other cats are not dogs and some dogs are not cats, although not true in fact, is equally consistent with what is stated in the premises. So too are the relationships shown in the other two diagrams. The conclusion asserted in our fallacious argument is No. 3—that all cats are dogs.

This happens not to be true, but we could easily substitute terms for A, B, and C in such a way that the conclusion was true in fact. For example—

> *All dogs are mammals,*
> *All collies are mammals,*
> *Therefore, all collies are dogs.*

The conclusion happens to be true, but the argument remains a wrong one, for the conclusion is not the only one which is consistent with what is stated in the premises. So we have a true conclusion supported by an unsound argument. This, of course, is always liable to happen. An unsound argument is not necessarily used to support wrong conclusions. The objection to it is that it does not prove its conclusions. The fact that an unsound argument may be used to support true conclusions gives us another form of the "diversion by irrelevant objection," for one may discredit the conclusions put forward by an adversary by showing that he has used an unsound argument in their support, even though his conclusions are true ones. A person against whom this device can be fairly used, however, does not deserve much sympathy.

This particular form of crooked thinking is called by logicians "the fallacy of the undistributed middle." It has this name because the term common to both premises, the "middle term" (in this case "mammals"), is not distributed over the whole class of mammals (that is, the word left out in front of it is "some" and not "all") in either of the places where it is used. Thus we have here again a piece of crooked thinking resulting from uncertainty as to whether "some" or "all" is implied.

It has been necessary to illustrate this form of fallacy by the ordinary trivial kind of illustration used in the textbooks, because if I had illustrated it by an argument of real significance in current controversy, there would have been danger of switching interest on to the controversy and away from the form of the argument. It is not, however, in such trivial questions that elementary errors of logic escape notice. No one would conclude from the fact that all cats and all dogs are mammals that, therefore, all cats are dogs, in however disguised a form this proposition was presented to them.

In order to demonstrate an argument of this kind which may be heard from reasonable and intelligent persons, we must take a subject matter about which such persons feel strongly. Instead of cats and dogs we may talk about C.I.O. leaders and Communists. The argument would then run:

[51]

All Communists are radicals,
All C.I.O. leaders are radicals,
Therefore, all C.I.O. leaders are Communists.

Even with such explosive subject matter, probably few people would fail to see the error if the argument were displayed in the fully dissected form we have used here. But if the argument were incomplete (as it generally is in practice), and if also its subject matter called out strong emotional reactions, then we should have the conditions which make possible and common the acceptance of this and grosser departures from logical thinking.

Actually the argument would take some such form as the following. "The C.I.O. leaders are the American agents for Communism, for they have the same radical ideas." "The C.I.O. leaders deny that they are identical with the Communists who have ruined Russia, but we shall only be able to believe in their sincerity when they have renounced the fallacies of radicalism." "If these men are not Communists, what are they? They admit that they are radicals. What are Communists if not radicals?" Shorn of emotionally toned words and other rhetorical devices, it will be seen that each of these arguments reduces to the form of the syllogism with an undistributed middle term that we have given above.

The Red Network, by Elizabeth H. Dilling, offers a classic example of sustained crooked thinking. This volume, compiled by a superpatriotic Midwestern lady, lists some thousands of Americans who belong to various organizations devoted to such causes as civil liberties, peace, better working conditions, opposition to race prejudice, and the like. The membership of some of these organizations includes a few Communists or sympathizers with the Soviet Union, and Mrs. Dilling therefore argues that because Communists believe in higher wages and oppose lynching, everyone who shares these beliefs is working under orders from Moscow. Actually, *The Red Network* lists as Russian agents not only such celebrated liberals as Mrs. Franklin D. Roosevelt and Mayor Fiorello H. LaGuardia but various assorted radicals who have associated themselves at one time or another with the defense of Leon Trotzky and have therefore been denounced by Communists as allies of Fascism. Those of my readers who care for diagram-making might amuse themselves by drawing two diagrams on the same principles that Mrs. Dilling had followed. The first diagram would show the relationship between members of peace organizations, labor unions, assorted charitable, reform, and social-service organizations on the one hand and Communist Party members on the other. The second diagram would show the relationship which would be necessary to make valid Mrs. Dilling's contention that every person listed in *The Red Network* is an agent of Moscow.

Before ending this chapter it may be well to mention two dishonest devices in argument which are known to every schoolboy—the argument in a circle and the argument which begs the question about which the dispute is taking place. These are somewhat less common in adult controversy than the tricks which have been already mentioned, but they are found sufficiently often to be worth a short examination.

The general form of the argument in a circle is: "If A then B, if B then C, if C then A." It is sometimes argued, for example, that human action is not free because what happens in a choice between two actions(let us say, between running away and standing one's ground in danger) is that the stronger impulse (to stand one's ground, for example) overcomes the other. If we further ask how we know that the impulse to stand one's ground was the stronger, the reply is that it must be because that is the behavior which actually took place. The argument then reduces to the form: the impulse to stand still overcame the impulse to run away because it was the stronger impulse; it was the stronger impulse because it overcame the other—an entirely circular argument.

We have already (in Chapter One) mentioned the crooked argument by "begging the question" or assuming what is to be proved. This cannot be done blatantly: if one began an argument by stating as an agreed principle the point that was in dispute, the trick would be too transparent to be successful. It can, however, be done by using a form of words which implies the conclusion, although not in an obvious way. The example given in Chapter One of the use of words involving moral judgments when a moral question is at issue is a fairly transparent trick, but it is not uncommon as an important part of a complicated argument. If a disputant wants to establish the guilt of an individual or a group of men, he is likely to use an argument in which he describes them as "scoundrels," "unprincipled blackguards," etc.

Another method of using the same trick is to assume what has to be proved in a definition. The ease with which this can be done is one of the reasons for the modern distrust (which we shall notice later) of the kind of reasoning in which definition plays a large part. In order that this trick may be used, it is not necessary that formal definition of the words used should take place. The question-begging definition may only be implied.

Let us suppose that A and B dispute as to whether Christians lead better lives than those who are not Christians. A maintains that they do, but in opposition to him B points to numerous persons who go to church and profess Christian beliefs but who drink too much, neglect their families, and lead otherwise discreditable lives. A, however, refuses to accept this as evidence against his contention on the ground that those who do such things are not "really" Christians. A's argument implies a definition of Christians which includes as one of the essential marks the leading of a virtuous life. The question in dispute is begged by the definition of a Christian which is implied by A.

Clearly one could prove a large number of propositions by a similar method. One could prove that all swans are white by refusing to count as a swan any bird that was not white. Some people are unwilling to admit that this is a crooked form of argument.

The word "Christian" is a much less definite one than "swan," and a definition which includes the leading of a virtuous life as one of the essential marks of a Christian is not unusual and quite legitimate, and if the definition be accepted, then the conclusion cannot be denied. This is true, and if the statement that all Christians lead virtuous lives is taken simply as a statement of how we are going to use the word "Christian," no important objection can be made against it. In the argument given above, however, A meant more than a statement about how he used words; he certainly meant to state a proposition about outside fact. This proposition was that those who possessed the external marks of being Christians (going to church, professing the Christian creed, etc.) also tended to possess the character of leading a virtuous life. This may well be true, but it cannot be established by the argument that A used, for he begged the question at issue by his definition.

Argument in a circle and begging the question are universally recognized as dishonest tricks in argument. In order to refute an opponent who uses one of them, it is therefore only necessary to show that the trick is being used. In order to do this it is sometimes necessary to put one's opponent's arguments in a simpler form so that the error may be more easily seen. Particularly is this the case when the question has been begged by choice of words or by definition.

CHAPTER FIVE

Tricks of Suggestion

IN popular speech these are sometimes called "hypnotic" tricks. They are, in fact, used to produce
the condition of trance known as the "hypnotic
state," in which the hypnotizer fixes his patient with
a steady gaze and in a firm, confident manner tells
him that he is falling asleep. We sometimes read that
powerfully persuasive orators "hypnotize their audiences" into believing what is required of them. That,
of course, can never be literally true. The hypnotic
trance is a condition startlingly different from the
alert state of everyday life, and an audience that was
literally hypnotized would attract as much attention
as one that was dead drunk. Such an expression must
only be understood as the same kind of inexact metaphor as when we speak of another audience being
"intoxicated with enthusiasm." So we shall prefer
the more exact technical psychological term and talk
of "tricks of suggestion."

The psychological fact of suggestion is the fact that
if statements are made again and again in a confident
manner, without argument or proof, then their hearers
will tend to believe them quite independently of their
soundness and of the presence or absence of evidence

for their truth. More particularly will his hearers tend to accept the suggestions of a speaker if he has what we may call "prestige"—the acknowledged dignity of authority possessed by senators, bishops, prize fighters, successful authors, and other famous men.

An orator using the method of suggestion relies then on three things: (1) repeated affirmation, (2) a confident, insistent method of speaking, and (3) prestige.

First, let us be clear as to exactly what we mean by "repeated affirmation." We may contrast two ways of trying to make somebody else agree with us. One is to put forward honestly the reasons we have for our belief. If we do this, we must be prepared also to consider his reasons for disagreeing with us and to weigh against each other the worth of his reasons and of our own. Obviously a laborious method, and one that is not likely to lead to a feeling of absolute certainty on the matter in dispute. It has the advantage that it is the one method which may help both disputants to some sight, however dim, of the truth.

Such an advantage will not weigh heavily in favor of this method in the minds of those who wish for quick results—who want a feeling of certainty rather than a knowledge of truth, and who prefer that people should act blindly and enthusiastically under their guidance rather than that they should decide calmly and wisely. For these, another method is open—that of simply saying the thing which is to be believed over and over again. This is "repeated affirmation."

No one could have told from first principles that mere repetition of the words expressing a statement would make the hearers tend to believe that statement. That is a fact which had to be discovered—the fact that may be described by the phrase "human suggestibility." It has been known as a matter of practice by those wishing to influence opinion even when they have never heard the words "suggestion" and "suggestibility." If we placard the walls of a town with notices which simply say, "Vote for Simpkins," that in itself will tend to make the voters vote for Simpkins although the notices do not give any reason for supposing that he is a better man than his rival Snooks. The notices rely on suggestion alone.

The suggestion is made more powerful if it can be delivered in speech and not merely in print, so Simpkins himself tours his constituency and makes speeches in which he says, "I shall win," and, "Sound and stable government can only be insured to the country by the victory of the X party." His speech would be monotonous if he merely said these things over and over again in the same words, so he says them over and over again in different words. "The country will be led to prosperity by our honored and trusted leader, John Smith," "The American people will never support the discredited Republican party or the wild experimentation of the Democrats," "Our country needs (and will now have) a period of government by men of sound principle." These phrases are quite differently worded, but they contain nothing but the two very simple ideas with which we started— "I shall win" and "Sound and stable government can only be insured to the country by the victory of the

X party." The orator is using the method of repetition although he repeats himself in different words partly to avoid monotony and partly to conceal the method actually used. A speech of this kind is like a piece of music made up of one or two short tunes which occur again and again with slight variations.

But the speaker does not rely merely on repetition. There are manners of repetition more successful than others. A halfhearted, hesitating kind of delivery has little suggestive effect. So the speaker develops the opposite manner of brazen confidence. Whatever doubts and hesitations and timidities he may feel are not allowed to appear in his manner. He thrusts out his chest, lifts up his head, and talks in a steady, loud voice. This is his confident manner, which is the second aid to success in suggestion. An inner feeling of certainty that one is right may be a valuable help to producing the manner, but is not essential to it. A practiced speaker who has learned the trick of the confident manner can put it on like a mask. A political candidate will find it a greater help to his success than any amount of expert knowledge on the work of government which he is proposing to undertake.

No political campaigner in American history has mastered these tricks more skillfully than President Roosevelt. During his 1936 campaign for re-election he resorted again and again to affirmations, to a confident manner of speaking, and to reliance on the prestige that his high office lent him. Speaking in Pittsburgh a few weeks before election he triumphantly proclaimed to a cheering audience of 50,000 people that jammed the local baseball park, "It's in the bag!" On the eve of election he delivered his famous "We have just begun to fight" speech in Madison Square Garden and since then he has often used the words "one third of the nation ill-housed, ill-clad, ill-fed"—phrases that have long since gone into the language.

A candidate for the presidency of the United States does not have to take hecklers into account. Also, he can exploit his prestige to great advantage. This applies equally to candidates for the office and to those running for re-election—as Alfred E. Smith learned to his cost in 1928. Accustomed to the rough and tumble of Tammany politics, Mr. Smith affected an even more colloquial speech than he uses habitually and his brown derby became his campaign emblem. He knew how to reply to hecklers and many of his speeches were almost impromptu affairs. The late Huey Long relied upon the same technique but since he confined his appeal to the poor whites of his native Louisiana and to the underprivileged section of the nation generally, he made great headway in those quarters. He ridiculed Mr. Roosevelt's patrician middle name, Delano, which he drawled out as slowly as possible in a scornful tone.

Mr. Roosevelt himself, however, never made the mistake of attempting to meet Huey Long on his own ground—any more than Herbert Hoover condescended to trade wisecracks with Al Smith. The man who speaks before a crowd of hostile hecklers proceeds quite differently from the man delivering a prepared address to a respectful audience. Likewise the campaigner who confines his efforts to the wrong side of the railway tracks will not get himself up in a cutaway coat, silk hat, and spats. But when a candidate for high office delivers a major address, dignity of speech and dress count ten. After all, people are more suggestible to those in high station than to anyone else.

As an example of the use of prestige, I will take a seller of patent medicines I saw in a market place a few years ago. He was introduced as professor of physiology at a well-known Northern university and a great authority on physical training. He mounted a tub and began by telling us that he did not generally speak from a tub but from his own Rolls-Royce. In fact, he was certainly not a professor of physiology, and there was no reason for supposing that he was the owner of a Rolls-Royce (an improbable combination, in any case). These were fictions designed to increase his prestige. Professors have a certain amount of prestige, and wealthy men (ownership of a Rolls-Royce implying wealth) have perhaps more. I did not wait to see how much medicine he succeeded in selling; probably not much. His technique of prestige magnification was not good. His manner lacked self-confidence, and he needed a shave. A shave would have done more toward bolstering up his prestige than his story of the Rolls-Royce.

Prestige by pure humbug is to be found elsewhere employed with more commercial success. There are a large number of pseudopsychological quacks who are advertised as "world-famous psychologists, authors, lecturers, and inspirational teachers." True, we have never heard of them before, but such an overwhelming list of qualifications creates a sufficient prestige to persuade foolish people to go to vague lectures on the powers of the subconscious and the training of our psychic vibrations, followed by twenty classes with fuller teaching at the nominal fee of $25. A widespread knowledge of the nature of suggestion ought to act as a safeguard against people being exploited by such methods of increasing prestige, and the spread of real education (which means the development of critical unsuggestible minds) should result in sending such people out of business and keeping the fee of $25 in their victim's pocket.

Prestige by false credentials may be successfully employed without any such elaborate method as this. The well-known trick of using obscure technical jargon in a discussion is often a device for acquiring undeserved prestige. The squire in *The Vicar of Wakefield* confuted his opponent by asking: "Whether do you judge the analytical investigation of the first part of my enthymem deficient secundum quoad, or quoad minus?"

This trick of mystifying one's opponent by technical jargon is not generally, of course, performed as blatantly as this, but unnecessary obscurity is a common feature of third-rate books on psychology and other sciences. Idleness and incompetence on the part of the authors is part of the explanation of this, but also it springs from the fact that this is the easiest

[63]

way to get a reputation for learning. The trick of intentional obscurity by jargon is, I think, used consciously and deliberately by the psychological quack lecturers I have mentioned above. It is unfortunately true that many people are more easily persuaded by what they cannot understand. There are some who would only believe in the scientific importance of the contentions of the first chapter of this book if I had expressed it by saying: "The function of verbalization is not only objective indication but also the production of conditioned endocrine responses."

It is not easy to find a satisfactory protection against this device. The use of a technical language not understandable to anyone who has not troubled to master it is a necessity in any branch of learning. It is a kind of intellectual shorthand which enables one to say in a sentence what could otherwise only be explained in many pages. When we meet obscurity in oral discussion, the best reply is to ask one's opponent to explain more simply what he means. If he cannot explain himself in simple language, even though he has the opportunity of doing so at great length, we may reasonably suspect him of not understanding what he means himself. It does not necessarily follow that he is using technical terms for prestige effect; he may only be incapable of expressing himself in any other way.

Obscurity in reading matter is more difficult to deal with. We cannot expect to be able to read advanced books on any subject without mastering first its technical vocabulary. Even with some mastery of a technical vocabulary, we find, however, many books partially incomprehensible. In my own subject, I should be inclined to guess that ten books are obscure because their authors are incompetent and muddleheaded or anxious for the prestige effects of obscurity, for every one that is obscure because it is dealing with really difficult matters that the utmost effort of the author could not make anything but difficult.

Let us take as examples of obscurity two passages, one from a first-rate authority on psychology and the other from an author who is not. The first is: "In the more purely instinctive reactions of still lower vertebrates, dyscritic differentiation alone probably suffices to permit of such saliency of the biologically important pattern as is needful to educe the appropriate response." Secondly we have: "In the spirit media are vested all experience and knowledge of all vibrations which are thoughts, and its vibrations of infinite velocity are expressed in the media of graduated molecularity at reduced speeds."

I suppose that to anyone not familiar with the shorthand language of scientific terminology these two passages seem about equally likely to mean nothing in particular. How then can we say that the first expresses as clearly as is possible in so short a space an important fact, while the second is (in my judgment, which may be wrong) mere vague mystification?

As to the first passage, the answer is easy. If we study psychology and physiology, we shall know its language and shall then be able to understand it and to express its meaning in simpler terms if we are willing to do so at much greater length. The second passage is less easy to deal with. We are driven back to an appeal to reasonable authority. My judgment that it means nothing in particular will be confirmed by most other students of the subject. We may all be wrong. The author may be struggling against a difficulty in thought which he can only overcome by the creation of a language of his own. The great philosopher Kant was obscure, and many of his contemporaries judged that, therefore, he was vague and meaningless. They were wrong. But on the whole it is more probable that what is judged to be mere vagueness and emptiness of thought by those who have been trained in overcoming the legitimate obscurities of technical language is really so. The number of books that are hopelessly vague and relatively empty of meaning is large; much larger than a charitable reader would wish to suppose.

There is no sure way to distinguishing them. There are certain writers whose books any student of the subject knows are of real value, whose obscurities must be overcome by effort on the part of the reader. The student knows also the names of a much larger number of others whose obscurities are not likely to be worth penetrating. None of us can hope to have this knowledge except in a very small field of learning. Outside that field we must rely on the judgment of others or else be prepared to waste a great deal of our own time.

Many of the tricks of dishonest argument which have been described earlier can be most easily carried through with a backing of prestige. A diversion (pp. 36–40), for example, can most easily be forced or a fallacy escape notice when a person of greater prestige is arguing against someone else with much less (let us say a professor against a student or a member of Congress against one of his constituents). Indeed the harmless protective device suggested against obscure language—that of confessing failure to understand and asking for explanation—may become a deadly weapon of dishonest argument in the hands of a man relying on his prestige. Let us suppose, for example, that a professor is asked an awkward question by one of his students and that he prefers a cheap victory to an honest discussion. He may say: "I am afraid, Mr. Smith, that I cannot understand what you mean. You are too subtle for me." It is clear that the impression left on the mind of an audience will be that the student must have been talking nonsense, for they cannot suppose that otherwise the professor would have been unable to understand him.

Perhaps the best way to counter this trick is one suggested by Schopenhauer. Like a jujitsu wrestler, instead of opposing the weight of his antagonist, the student may give way to it, in order thus to overthrow him. He may say, for example: "Your failure to understand me must be my fault. Let me explain myself more clearly." He can then explain what he means so fully and clearly that the simplest onlooker

[67]

must understand that he has made his point. Obviously the same trick can be used by a Congressional candidate against a questioner, with the additional advantage that the questioner will have no opportunity of countering the attack.

Other controversial devices depending on suggestion are those in which the answer is in some way dictated by the question. Most simply this happens when the question suggests its own answer, as: "Surely you accept the principles of the Reformation?" or "You accept the principles of the Reformation, don't you?" If the person questioned is showing himself resistant to suggestion, this method can be reversed and a question asked which implies the opposite answer to that required; the questioner frames his question so as to appear to be trying to force the answer "No," when he really wants his opponent to answer "Yes."

A variant of the same method is the well-known trick of asking a question so framed that any direct answer to it will imply an admission damaging to your case. "Will agriculture benefit by the increased prices which will follow the processing tax?" Clearly, either of the answers "Yes" or "No" implies the admission that such taxation would raise food prices, which the person disputing may not be willing to admit. The same end can be attained by asking many different things as a complicated question demanding a single answer, as, for example, "Do you admit that the enemy have murdered their prisoners, bombed defenseless towns, fired on the Red Cross, and sunk hospital ships? Yes or no." Plainly the person questioned might wish to answer "Yes" to some of these questions, "No" to others, and to make some qualifications to his answers to others. Either of the answers invited will land him in many admissions he does not want to make.

It is obvious that the first trick must be met by refusing to be influenced by the suggestion, and the second and third by dividing up the question and answering different parts separately. So obvious is this that one might wonder why such tricks are ever successful. It is because the tricks are used with an overbearing technique of suggestion. Without that they would have no force, and with it the correct reply may be almost impossibly difficult.

The real remedy required is to liberate oneself from the influence of suggestion. This is partly a matter of self-education, but all of us find ourselves sometimes in situations where the forces of suggestion are acting strongly on us. Let us suppose that we are being questioned by a dignified person in a position of real authority (one who can send us to prison, let us say) who adopts an overbearing manner and these controversial tricks. We can respond by using just as much of the confident manner ourselves as is safe. In addition to this there are psychological devices for reducing the effects of his suggestion. We can, for example, under our breath make suggestions to ourselves undermining the dignity of our questioner and establishing our own before the examination begins. Or, since much of the prestige effect of our questioner

[69]

depends on his clothes, we may find effective the device of picturing to ourselves what he would look like with nothing on. Any such device reducing the weight of his prestige will help us to adopt the right method of dealing with any of these tricks that he may bring against us.

We have described examples of prestige suggestion based on false credentials. It may have better foundations, and still be harmful. Titles of distinction, such offices as that of judge, and a university degree are all props to prestige and can all be abused. My own university degrees have been honestly earned by hard work. I may, however, use them in exactly the same way as the imaginary professorship and the Rolls-Royce of the patent-medicine seller: if I do, I am as much to blame as he was. It is true that I can claim a certain amount of reasonable authority. I have read a large number of books and I have performed some experiments designed to find out new facts of psychology. I can, therefore, say authoritatively what is inside those books and what were the results of my experiments. There my reasonable authority ends. If I exploit any prestige I have to say authoritatively things on which I have no certain knowledge, I can rely on the fact that human suggestibility will make a large number of people willing to believe me. If I said in an impressive tone of voice, on my authority as a psychologist, that there are or that there are not such things as ghosts, or that our souls are or are not immortal, I could succeed in influencing a great many suggestible people, although a moment's reflection

[70]

should convince them that I have exactly the same right to an opinion on such subjects as they have themselves and no more. Such exploitation of prestige is as far from straight thinking as is the prestige suggestion of the politician, the racing tipster, the patent-medicine seller, and the quack healer.

We should be inclined to distrust all suggestion by prestige and not merely that based on false credentials. The prestige of professors and learned men has been used to crush many movements of scientific discovery at their beginning. The authoritative voice of the learned world put off the acceptance of Harvey's discovery of the circulation of the blood for a whole generation, as it had previously delayed the acceptance of Copernicus' discovery of the earth's motion. Lister's discovery of the use of antiseptics in surgery was similarly opposed by established medical authority within the memory of men now living. In our own days we have heard the thunders of established authority against the revolutionary psychological discoveries of the great Viennese psychotherapist, Professor Freud.

Remember that the opposition to these things did not come from men who could say: "Having thoroughly investigated the work of these so-called discoverers and repeated their observations and experiments I have found that their conclusions are wrong." That would be an appeal to reasonable authority. On the contrary, what they said was in effect this: "As an authority on this subject, I know without any detailed examination that these results are absurd."

While it is not easy to distinguish in practice between an appeal to an authority which is reasonably grounded and one which is not, the difference is of vital importance. If a great physicist announces an experimental result of an investigation in gravitation, we may reasonably accept his opinion on his authority even if we cannot repeat his experiment. Not only can we do this because we consider that he is a reliable experimenter, but also because other workers will be able to test his results, and they could not stand such investigation if they were wrong. If, however, he gives us his opinion on the immortality of the soul or on the freedom of the human will, we should attach little weight to his authority and we ought not to quote it in argument. He has the same data for drawing his conclusions on this subject as everyone else.

Let us call an argument based on the latter kind of authoritative statement an "appeal to mere authority," contrasting it with an appeal to reasonable authority. There was a time when the commonest argument in intellectual dispute was the appeal to mere authority, and it was considered sufficient to support a statement by saying: "Aristotle says so-and-so," without considering whether Aristotle had a better reason for saying what he did than we have for saying the opposite. Still, some of us are content to settle disputed questions by appealing in exactly the same way to the authority of Marx, of St. Paul, or even of the latest speaker we have heard at a lecture.

A common appeal to mere authority is the statement: "Everybody says so-and-so." Just as with Aristotle, Marx, and St. Paul, we should ask whether there is any good reason for supposing that, in the particular matter under discussion, "everybody" is likely to be right. So also when we meet the common appeal to the authority of the past: "This has always been believed," we should ask ourselves whether, in this particular matter, our ancestors had sound reasons for their opinion or whether we have fuller knowledge which entitles us to revise their judgments.

While reasonably grounded learned authority can be a force of great value and is indeed our principal protection against the cruelties of commercial exploitation by humbug and quackery, yet it has been too often in the past a force opposing the advance of knowledge. Its power to do this (as also the power of the quackery which it should suppress) can only be rendered harmless when men lose their subservience to prestige suggestion. The practical aim of the discussion of prestige suggestion in the present chapter is to help my readers to liberate themselves from its power by recognizing its nature. Those who understand the workings of suggestion will be less influenced by the suggestion method of presenting opinions.

Already, I think, prestige suggestion is beginning to lose its force, and the pronouncements of "authorities" now meet with more critical intelligence and less humble acceptance than was once the case. I have heard a professor deplore the fact that modern students no longer reverence their professors. God forbid that they should! It is part of the business of a professor to see that his students remain in a condition of critical alertness toward what he tells them instead of falling into this reverence which is the emotion accompanying the acceptance of prestige suggestion. Dr. Rivers of Cambridge used to say: "When students no longer contradict me flatly to my face, I shall know that I have grown old." That is the spirit we want through all education—not teachers who use their prestige to force meek acceptance of what they say, but those who retain to the end of their days the spirit of students, always ready to learn more, and expecting from those whom they have to teach, argument, contradiction, and above all, the impartial testing of the truth by experiment.

After we have said all we can against the use of tricks of suggestion, it remains true that in public speaking some use of them is unavoidable. If anyone is giving a public address and decides, in the interests of straight thinking, that he will not speak in a confident voice and never make any point more than once, he will not be a success as a speaker. His audience will be bored and is more likely to be impressed with his incompetence than with his honesty. It would not even be practicable for a speaker to get rid of all prestige effects by persuading his chairman to tell the plain truth about his complete lack of competence to make any contribution worth while to the subject he is speaking on.

We can (and should) do all we can to reduce suggestibility by directing education toward independence of judgment and by showing the hollowness of the greater number of prestige pretensions, but when we come to speak in public we must address our audience firmly and confidently, using the method of varied repetition and under the protection of so much of a halo of prestige as the chairman sees fit to provide us with.

We should do this not in order that we may exploit the suggestibility of our audience, but because it is the only efficient way of public speaking. Suggestion, however, will follow whether we intend it or not; our audiences will tend to accept what we say to them quite independently of any reasonable ground for supposing it to be true. Intellectual honesty makes, therefore, certain demands on a public speaker. He must never say in a public speech what he would not be prepared to maintain in private argument with none of the apparatus of suggestion at his command. He must not use confident affirmation as a substitute for argument in order to make his audience accept a doubtful proposition. He must not represent as certain a proposition which he thinks is only probably true. He must never use the politician's common trick of crushing an honest objector by a dishonest reply with nothing but tricks of suggestion to support it.

Intellectual honesty is not necessarily incompatible with public speaking, and there is no reason why those who value intellectual integrity should leave all the public speaking of the world to be done by the tricksters and the exploiters of suggestibility. Yet the atmosphere of the public platform is not favorable to intellectual honesty, and there is every reason why a public speaker should examine his conscience carefully in the light of what he knows about the mechanism of suggestion. His best protection, however, is an alert, critical, and relatively unsuggestible audience, fully aware of the nature of tricks of suggestion and of the difference between them and honest argument.

CHAPTER SIX

Habits of Thought

THE ease and the pleasure with which our minds
slip into habitual lines of thought is one of the
characters of human thinking used by orators who
wish to exploit our power of crooked thinking. Those
of us who speak in public know how easy it is to find
some phrase which just coincides with the thought
habits of our audience. We know when we have got
such a phrase by the applause which follows. A skillful orator begins his speech by many such phrases.
He refers to "the glorious institutions of our great
country" (applause), to "the sound common sense of
the American people" (more applause), and to their
"unconquerable spirit" (still more applause). By this
time he has produced in his audience an attitude of
willingness to accept what he says. He can now go on
to say things which earlier their thought habits would
have led them to reject. He can say, for example, that
we have nothing left of Liberty except the Statue, or
that the glory of our nation is being dimmed by our
lawlessness or bureaucracy. And the audience go on
accepting what he says. The resistance which would
certainly have been shown against these statements if
he had started with them has been broken down by

this simple device of beginning with easily accepted statements.

The same device may be used by a quack psychological healer. He tells his audience that the mind has greater power over the body, which is true. He goes on to illustrate this power by stories which may also be true. He may tell, for example, of people who seemed to be dumb or paralyzed who became suddenly well under the influence of some emotional crisis. He may even illustrate this power by some simple experiments. When his audience are in a receptive state of mind he goes on to tell them the falsehoods which are the real object of the whole discourse. He tells them that he has a method by which all their illnesses, physical or mental, may be cured, which will be communicated in small classes. If the trick has succeeded and members of his audience have gone on believing the speaker because the first things he said seemed to them to be obviously true, they will be $25 poorer and probably no better in health.

So if we hear a succession of statements, A, B, C, and D, which our minds accept readily and with enthusiasm, we must still be on guard against accepting a fifth statement, E. A, B, C, and D may only have been ground bait intended to produce the habit of swallowing everything the speaker says. E may conceal the hook.

Our caution, however, should extend even further than this. The ease and readiness with which we accept A, B, C, and D is no guarantee that even they are true. The laws of habit formation hold in the mind as they do in the body. Thoughts we have thought often pass through our minds with increasing ease until they appear obvious. Emotions that have been called up in connection with particular thoughts are aroused more easily by those thoughts until the connection between emotion and thought appears to us to be a necessary one. So an appreciation of psychology should lead us to reject the old statement of the philosophers that what we cannot doubt must be true. What we cannot doubt may simply be based on a very deeply rooted thought habit and may well be false.

Our ancestors, for example, found themselves unable to doubt that the earth stood still while the sun moved round it every day. We ourselves have found it equally difficult to doubt that there is an exact meaning in the statement that two events in different places occurred at the same time. Yet both of these convictions were wrong, and were simply based on deeply grounded habits of thought. One of these sets of thought habits was broken by Copernicus when he showed that the facts were better explained by supposing that instead of the sun moving round the earth, the earth rotated on its axis. The other set was broken by Einstein when he revolutionized physics by bringing forward his special theory of relativity.

We all have a newspaper acquaintance with Einstein's theory of relativity, so I can safely take from it another example of the power of thought habits to hinder the mind from reaching new truth. In his general theory of relativity, Einstein made a statement offensive to our "common sense" (that is, to our habits of thought) by saying that space in the neighborhood of matter was non-Euclidean. This means that in such space the angles of a triangle would not add up to two right angles.

Now, the proposition that the three angles of every triangle together make up two right angles is a proposition in Euclid, but Euclid himself recognized that the proposition was a peculiar one. It was essential to nearly everything he proved afterward, but itself rested on another proposition which could not be proved. So he treated this as an axiom, although it was not self-evident. Other geometers since Euclid's time have tried to prove this proposition, but no sound proof has been found, and it was finally decided that a sound proof was impossible. So other mathematicians worked out what they called "non-Euclidean geometries," based on the assumption that the sum of the angles of triangles was less or was more than two right angles. If we make either of these assumptions, we can base a whole geometry on it. Such a geometry may not be true of the space we know, but it will be self-consistent. It will be true of a possible space if not of the space in which we live.

Now it might be asked (and frequently was asked): "What is the good of that kind of speculation? If we know that the angles of triangles do add up to two right angles what is the good of assuming they don't?" The answer was: "The question is not whether they *do* add up to two right angles but whether they *must*. If they must, then the conclusions of Euclid would hold for all possible universes, but if it only happens that they do, and our conviction that they must has no better foundation than our habits of thought, then it is quite worth while to find out what are the consequences of the opposite assumption." The important practical result of these speculations was that they made possible the acceptance of Einstein's theory (which was true and which had verifiable practical consequences). If people had remained convinced that every triangle must obey Euclid's law they could not have reached the general theory of relativity. Insight into new truth was made possible by the destruction of an old thought habit.

Few of the thought habits we may be asked to question will ever appear so obvious to us as the conviction that Euclidean geometry must be true. The apparent obviousness of a conviction is no guarantee of its truth. Once we are convinced of that, we should be prepared boldly to experiment in questioning the apparent truths based on our habits of thought.

The physical theory of relativity is a very useful example of the danger of thought habits closing our minds to new truth, for it is in the fact of relativity in its wider sense that this danger is greatest. We all of us tend to judge problems from one particular standpoint, the one determined by our own conditions of life. We are inhabitants of our own particular country, with a particular religious and moral tradition, and we are inclined to forget how many of our judgments are simply relative to this single standpoint and are not absolute.

It is only when we begin to study comparative religions and comparative codes of morals that we begin to see to what extent our own opinions about right and wrong and about other matters are not scientific truths (for these are true for all persons under all conditions), but are judgments whose truth is entirely relative to the particular point of view from which they were made. By accustoming our minds to comparative studies and by forming the habit of trying to look at problems in a manner which discounts our own point of view, we can to some extent escape from this relativity. Such statements, for example, as that "the heathen are wicked folk without law or religion," that "Americans are dollar chasers," or that "Europeans are degenerate," will be seen to be statements made entirely from a limited point of view and with no objective validity at all.

Particularly in international affairs, we must remember this relativity of our point of view. Most of us would be able to judge a dispute between Rumania and Jugoslavia more objectively and scientifically than we would judge a dispute between the United States and Japan—always provided we had access to the facts. But until we can see and feel the other side's case as well as our own, our judgments cannot possibly even approach scientific validity. Most people seem not to realize this, and after the last war the Allied Powers felt they were capable not merely of acting as prosecuting attorneys against their late enemies, but as their judges. Now a judge has to make objective, universally true judgments, and this could plainly only be done by someone as detached from that dispute as Americans should be from one between Rumania and Jugoslavia.

An instructive experiment is to take a statement expressing our own point of view on a subject on which we have well-developed thought habits; then, making no other alteration, to change the particular matters with which it deals to others which are similar but about which we have different thought habits. Now we can consider the statement with its new subject matter and see whether our attitude toward it remains the same. So we judge how far our attitude toward the original statement possessed objective or scientific validity, and how far it was acceptable to us merely because it fitted in with our thought habits.

During a war, for example, we read with strong approval of its author's honesty and courage the writings of an enemy national living in a neutral country expressing opinions unfavorable to his own country. Perhaps our judgment is right, but, in order to be sure that we are not being unduly influenced by our own thought habits, let us consider what would be (or what, in fact, has been) our attitude toward members of our own country expressing in similar conditions opinions unfavorable to ourselves. Or we applaud our own Government's firm action in holding responsible for the death of a murdered American official an alien Government through whose neglect of precautions for his safety the murder took place. Let us consider what our attitude would be toward similar demands made by another country in similar circumstances (let us say, by the old Austrian empire against Serbia when an Austrian archduke is killed by a Serbian bomb). There is no limit to the field for such intellectual experimentation—Communist executions of Trotzkyites, Nazi executions of Communists, Franco's executions of Republicans, British executions of Indian Nationalists, the execution of Sacco and Vanzetti by the Commonwealth of Massachusetts.

The result of the experiment will not, of course, always be to lead us to revise our opinions. Very often, however, it will. Always it should help us to rid our judgments of that element in them which is due to our thought habits and which is relative only to our own limited point of view, and to replace such imperfect opinions by judgments which more nearly approach the ideal of impartiality.

We may try this with the following passage from a speech which I found by chance at the back of a press cutting. It is a stirring passage, so it is a suitable subject for an experiment to determine how much of its stir (if any) is independent of the thought and emotional habits it arouses:

> *Unless we play our part as an Imperial race there is nothing but disaster in front of the human race. (Applause.) With the effervescence that is going on in the world today, the only force to my mind which can maintain the ideal of ordered freedom is the 70,000,000 of the true American nation and the 70,-000,000 there or thereabouts, of the white race of the British Empire. These 140,000,000 people, speaking the English tongue, reading the English Bible and the English Shakespeare, with ideas which were*

embodied originally in Magna Charta—these people with a common background of civilization have to share the responsibility for maintaining civilization among the 1800 or 1900 million people on the globe.

Now we are undoubtedly moved by this speech, but before we take our feelings at their face value we must remember that it is rather easy for us (as for other people) to form habits of thinking of ourselves as the chosen civilizers of all the rest of the world, and to form habits of responding with exalted emotions to speeches expressing this destiny. So to test the real worth of this passage we will try it again in a setting in which we have formed different habits.

At a review in 1914 of the German army at Potsdam, the Kaiser said:

Unless we play our part as an Imperial race there is nothing but disaster in front of the human race. With the effervescence that is going on in the world today, the only force to my mind which can maintain the ideal of ordered freedom is the 65,000,000, there or thereabouts, of the German Empire, and the 11,000,000 German-speaking members of the Austrian Empire. These 76,000,000 people, speaking the German tongue, reading the German Bible and the German Goethe—these people with a common background of Kultur *have to share the responsibility for maintaining civilization among the 1800 or 1900 million people on the globe.*

That, you will notice, is the same passage as before, put in a different setting. The setting has been changed to one in which we have different thought habits. Our reaction too is different. Instead of a dig-

[85]

nified statement of imperial responsibility, it sounds like an expression of national megalomania. How would the original passage have sounded to an impartial visitor from Mars?

Even the things about which we feel most certain (and perhaps rightly feel certain) have been questioned, and it may not be a bad thing for us to hear these questionings so that our deepest beliefs may be based on reasoned and critical conviction and not merely on thought habits. Christian believers may read the attacks of Nietzsche, and good constitutionalists may read the writings of Marx, Kropotkin, and Lenin. They will experience the uncomfortable sensation of an attempt to shake long-founded and deeply based thought habits. Perhaps those who are old are right to protect themselves from such an uncomfortable process, but those who are young and have the necessary flexibility of mind could profit by it. Their opinions may not be reversed, but they will no longer be merely based on thought habits which have never been questioned. They will be something stronger and better, the reasonable convictions of free minds. Those whose attitude toward what they regard as "subversive" literature is simply that it must be suppressed (by force if necessary) show little faith in the truth of the beliefs they are trying to protect.

We have in ordinary speech a word for expressing the feelings that are aroused in us when something presented to us breaks across cherished mental habits. We say we are "shocked"; and we resent being shocked. We believe in a censorship of plays, books, films, and wireless talks which will save us from any danger of being shocked. People who seem deliberately to write in order to shock us, writers such as Ibsen, Bernard Shaw, and Upton Sinclair, we are careful not to read. But why should we be so tender to our mental habits? Such writers do us a great service (the service done to the science of physics by the writers on non-Euclidean geometry) of forcing us to question our old beliefs so that we may freely and intelligently choose what is sound in them and reject the rest, and thus have our minds prepared for seeing new and unfamiliar truths. Most people do not need protection from being shocked. They need to be shocked a great deal more than they are.

There are a large number of problems it is impossible effectively to put before most people because they have so many thought habits in connection with them that they resent any questioning of them. "What changes (if any) ought we to make in the institution of marriage, or in the institution of private property?" "Ought we to control the size of our families?" "What ought to be our attitude toward those individuals who love members of their own and not of the opposite sex?" or "Is the New Deal a failure?" These are all questions which merely to raise in public is to set in action thought habits connected with such strong emotions that reasonable discussion and reasonable decision are quite impossible. Yet there should be no question reasonable people dare not ask, no thought too shocking to think if we are to regulate our affairs wisely.

Nor does the evil of keeping our minds closed to some possible lines of thought end with the social misfortune that there are some questions we can never decide wisely because we cannot think about them reasonably. We are learning more and more to recognize that people lead dwarfed and impoverished mental lives because there are parts of their own characters they dare not face, particularly the forces which belong to the life of love. We have comfortable little habits of thought which conceal from us the terrific forces of our instinctive natures, and these are treated by us as something alien and to be fought against when they ought to be recognized as our own and brought under our wise control. We smack our children when they ask us questions which we regard as improper or put them off with lies about storks and gooseberry bushes in order to preserve their innocence. Then we wonder why they are psychoneurotic and morbidly afraid at the stage of becoming grown up. We have ourselves destroyed their innocence by implanting habits of fear and evasion on a subject about which thought should be as free and unafraid as about any other. The reading of the works of Professor Freud has shocked many people out of such dangerous fears into a condition of mental liberation and mental health.

We must not suppose, of course, that we have escaped the danger of being imprisoned by our thought habits merely by giving up our old habits of thought which are much the same as everybody else's and starting new ones of our own. The unorthodox and

[88]

unconventional are in just as much danger of finding their minds closed to new truth by the persistence of their old habits of thought as are the orthodox and the conventional. They too have just the same need of being occasionally shaken out of their thought habits so that they may retain flexibility of mind. We have taken Bernard Shaw as an example of a writer who questions orthodox and conventional thought habits. Similarly we might take G. K. Chesterton as a writer whose function it is to question the thought habits of those who are unorthodox and unconventional.

The worst danger of all which threatens those who have rejected commonly accepted habits of thought is that they should form the habit of disbelieving things merely because other people believe them. This is what we mean by "crankiness." A "crank" is not a person free from thought habits, but one who has formed a thought habit which is at least as likely to hide the truth from him as is the opposite habit of accepting what is commonly believed.

It should be one of the aims of education to produce a quality that we may describe as "flexibility of mind," an ability to try out new ways of thinking and to make unfamiliar assumptions. This means that we must be able at will to put on one side our old thought habits. The mathematicians had thought habits based on the fact that the angles of all the triangles they had ever met had added up to two right angles, but they were able to ask themselves: "Suppose they hadn't, what would follow?" So we must keep for ourselves the power of intellectual experimentation. We see everywhere men carrying out work for wages or salary. We must ask ourselves: "Is this a necessary law, or can we imagine a form of society in which the monetary motive would not be the dominant one and yet in which the world's work would be done?" We are accustomed to a particular form of the marriage relationship. We must ask: "Is this the only possible one? Would other kinds of relationship be better or worse in securing the ends for which marriage exists?"

Clearly it is neither desirable nor possible to get rid of all thought habits. Such an aim would be absurd. The formation of thought habits is as inevitable as the formation of bodily habits and just as useful. But we must be ready continually to revise them. Thought habits once serviceable may prevent us from attaining to new truths. We differ from the lower animals in the possession of a rich and complicated brain. This is an instrument to give flexibility and adaptability to our behavior. If we allow ourselves merely to become creatures of habit, we become automatic and mechanical like the lower animals. We are allowing our brains to degenerate into mere mechanisms when they were meant for plasticity and change. It is like using a razor for digging the ground.

Astronomers tell us that the human race has many million years more to spend on this globe if it does not destroy itself by wars. It is only by unceasing flexibility of mind that we can continue to adapt ourselves to our ever-changing environment. Inflexibility of mind will lead to the extermination of the human race.

CHAPTER SEVEN

Tabloid Thinking

S OME of the methods of crooked thinking we have studied are rooted in a character of much human thinking which it will be worth while now to describe and name. Most true statements about complicated matters of fact cannot be summed up in a few words. To describe the effect of a protective tariff on the price of a commodity or on employment or the part played by sex in mental growth would require many words, many qualifying clauses, many distinctions between different cases, and many uncertainties. The majority of men, however, will have none of these complications. They feel that they have mastered the matter when they can reduce such a complicated body of knowledge to a simple formula with all the qualifications, distinctions, and uncertainties left out. They can sum up the effect of tariffs in such a phrase as "Processing taxes mean higher food prices" or "High tariffs make high wages." As to sex, Professor Freud has brought forward a body of doctrine complicated and guarded enough to give exercise to the most highly developed brain. Most of those who talk about his work, however (and these not all persons deficient in education), are quite content to sum it up simply as "Everything is sex."

Let us call this tendency "tabloid thinking." We find it is a widespread reaction to the complications of actual fact. Darwin's complicated and beautiful theory of the course of evolution was popularly reduced to the simple formula: "Men are descended from monkeys." This is not as bad as the common idea that the difficult mathematical physics of Einstein's theory of relativity is adequately summed up in the phrase: "Everything is relative." What science has discovered about the values of different kinds of food is similarly summed up in tabloid form, as: "Milk is nourishing," "Jam contains calories," and "Lettuces are rich in vitamins."

Observation of this tendency to eliminate all complications from statements before they are accepted explains the prevalence of the substitution of "all" for "some" (Chapter Two), the occasional ignoring of the undistributed middle (pp. 47–53), and the readiness to accept an extension of one's propositions (pp. 33–5). In all these cases the extreme proposition is the less complicated one, and therefore the one that we are prone to accept by our tendency to tabloid thinking.

A man, for example, begins to argue against the teachings of Freud. He will almost certainly begin to attack the view that "everything is sex." His own tabloid thinking has led him quite unwittingly to begin by inviting his opponent into the trap of the extension. His opponent may be better informed on the matter and try to explain which activities Freud thinks are related to sex and which he does not. This, however, is of no interest to the first speaker and he escapes by protesting that his opponent is too "learned" or too "subtle" for him. He protests that he is a plain man and that nothing will convince him that art, romantic love, and religion are just sex, which is generally agreed by everybody to be the teaching of Freud. Thus he entrenches himself in his tabloid thinking, and if the dispute takes place before an audience, he can generally be sure of having their sympathy, for his opponent will seem to be a person trying to make himself out to be too clever and who makes serious argument impossible by throwing doubt on what everyone knows to be true.

The popular controversialist has indeed a serious complaint against those who do not accept the tabloids of thought ordinarily current, because these are the agreed postulates for popular discussion. "American institutions are the finest in the world," "The Germans were responsible for the World War," "The higher critics tried to prove that the Bible was not true, but their conclusions are now out of date," "The welfare of a nation is based on the sanctity of its home life," "The Socialists wish to reduce all men to a dull uniformity." These are samples of the tabloid postulates of newspaper controversy. Without them, such controversy could not be carried on. Yet there is not one of them that can reasonably either be

[93]

denied or affirmed: they are simple statements on a number of matters about which the truth could hardly be told in less than several pages.

A statement expressed in tabloid form has the great practical advantage that it can be easily remembered and easily passed from one person to another. It is, therefore, easy for belief in it to be increased by the force of "suggestion" (Chapter Five). No kind of suggestion is stronger than the conviction that "Everybody says so-and-so." I was living in a village during an attack of influenza when word was passed from one back garden to another: "Bananas are so nourishing." Neither proof nor authority was demanded. Whoever heard these words went off to buy bananas for those who were in bed. Apparently lettuces, bread crumbs, or even boiled rats could have been fitted into the formula with equal effect. This tendency to accept any tabloid statement is being exploited by the advertiser who prints: "Snooks' mixture cures your cold."

A tabloid statement expressed in a fixed form of words which is handed from one person to another may be called a "slogan." A successful slogan may possess great power in directing the behavior of a large number of people in one direction. No complicated statement of the doctrines of Rousseau could have been as effective in directing the French Revolution as the slogan "Liberty, fraternity, equality." Now this slogan is obviously a tabloid. It is a very simple statement which would need a complicated expansion to mean anything exactly. Such an expansion

[94]

of "liberty" would need to explain what the people were and what they were not to be free to do; of "fraternity" to explain with whom they were to be fraternal (not aristocrats or enemies of their country); of "equality," in what respects they were to be equal. Yet such an expanded account would not serve any of the purposes of the slogan: that it should be readily accepted in its entirety, easily remembered, and able to stimulate a large number of people to similar action.

The use of slogans as a method of influencing people is by no means unreasonable. A skillful leader of men, however complicated were his own thought processes, would need to express his doctrines in tabloid form for them to be widely accepted, and, for the purposes of mass action, this could most conveniently be done by inventing slogans. Thus the second Russian revolution was directed not by a preaching of the subtleties of Marx to the people, but by the slogan "All power to the soviets." Perhaps the earliest forms of the Creeds were the slogans of the early Christians. Slogans can reasonably and properly be used to stir people to action but not to induce belief.

Probably there is no single explanation of tabloid thinking. There is the difficulty of grasping a complex proposition. The most finely developed brain reaches at some point the limit of the complexity it can grasp. With the majority of men, this limit is reached rather early. Long before it is reached, however, mental idleness steps in, making us tend to accept mental food well below the limits of our digestion. It is easier to

[95]

believe that Lenin was a thoroughly bad man than to accept a dispassionate estimate of all the sides of his character. So through idleness or indifference such a tabloid opinion is accepted even by those easily capable of making a more complex judgment if they chose to make the necessary mental exertion. Then we have seen how easily tabloid thinking expressed in a slogan can be adapted for various socially useful ends, as well as being convenient to remember.

There is, however, a much more important reason for tabloid thinking than any of these. It is that tabloid thinking gives us a consistent practical attitude toward things. During the war, it was commonly believed that the Germans were altogether evil—they sank hospital ships and lifeboats escaping from sinking vessels, bombed defenseless towns and hospitals, mutilated or murdered prisoners, falsified news, and even boiled down human bodies for the manufacture of fat. If anyone during the war questioned or denied even a single one of these items, he would certainly have been labeled a "pro-German." "What! you don't believe that the U-boats sink escaping lifeboats. How can you defend those barbarians? I know a man whose brother has a friend who saw with his own eyes a large cauldron in which human bodies were being boiled down for fat. The world won't be a fit place to live in until we've completely smashed them."

This last sentence explains the whole process of thought. It is not simply a diversion from one charge against the enemy to a different one. It is also a defense of a simplified picture of the enemy as evil, and therefore as something which must be vigorously fought against. In a war, one is engaged in the practical activity of fighting against the enemy. Any belief which makes one fight more strenuously is a serviceable one. From the same practical point of view, any belief which makes one fight less strenuously is undesirable. The conduct of one's enemies, like the conduct of oneself, is, in fact, mixed bad and good. But while belief in the bad strengthens our hands in fighting, belief in the good side of our enemies' characters would weaken our fighting efforts. So we accept the oversimplified tabloid picture of our enemies as evil, because that is the most useful picture for action, not because it is true.

We have a similar oversimplified picture of the character of, let us say, Lenin. Anyone who pointed out the historically accurate fact that one of Lenin's favorite amusements was playing with children or that he was a habitually merry man, would certainly be suspected of being a pro-Bolshevik (*i.e.* of having similar oversimplified tabloid beliefs favorable to the Bolsheviks), although neither love of children nor merriment is really inconsistent with the harsh and unlovely aspects of Lenin's character. But they spoil the perfection of the picture of Lenin as a person to be hated and fought against. They are unserviceable to conduct.

Indeed, it is not only in wars and revolutions that one finds this kind of tabloid thinking in which all perfection tends to be attributed to one's own side and all evil to the enemy. In elections it is very noticeable;

[97]

while the candidates on one side appear as models of all the civic and domestic virtues, those on the other are regarded as incompetent, untrustworthy, and evil persons. Here too action is required, and action must be simple although thought may be complex. One must vote on one side or the other: so to avoid the crippling condition of inaction the mind tends to pile up certainties in one direction in the form of tabloid estimates of the characters of the two parties.

Even in sport a similar tendency is found. A supporter of Cambridge, looking at a photograph of the Oxford cricket eleven, is reported by C. E. Montague to have said: "Look at them! The hangdog expressions! The narrow, ill-set Mongol eyes! The thin, cruel lips! Prejudice apart, would you like to meet that gang in a quiet place on a dark night?" Here no action is required except that of supporting wholeheartedly one's own side. Even that, however, can be done most comfortably by tabloid judgments. It is easier to be wholeheartedly "for" one side and "against" the other if we attribute all the virtues to the one and all the vices to the other.

So in history and novel reading too we fall into this kind of tabloid thinking. We make this partition of the vices and the virtues, for example, between the Catholics and Protestants at the time of the Reformation, between Loyalists and Insurgents in modern Spain, and even between Sioux and Hurons when we read Fenimore Cooper's novels.

Education has, in the past, often fostered the tendency to tabloid thinking instead of trying to combat

[98]

it.) Let us, for example, cast our minds back to the fragments of early history we retain from our school days. We were taught to regard its principal figures as either "bad" or "good" men. Thus Nero, Richard III of England, and Aaron Burr were "bad"—not merely bad "on the whole" but in all respects—oppressive, cruel, and tyrannical in their public lives with no redeeming features in their home lives. Edward III of England, Abraham Lincoln, and the Pilgrim Fathers, on the other hand, were equally uncompromisingly "good." Perhaps we know now that competent historians do not indorse such drastic judgments and that the best modern history books for schools (I believe) do not contain them. Our first reaction toward those who "whitewash" Richard III is uncomfortable indignation. We feel that they are the sort of people who try to get notoriety by questioning what everyone knows to be true.

Outside history, we similarly learned that Shakespeare was a great poet, and, if it was not actually taught, the tabloid proposition that all he wrote was perfect was at least implied. So the same shocked indignation has often greeted those who have tried intelligently to separate the fine grain from the chaff in Shakespeare's writing. In popular tabloid thinking, Shakespeare was "good" like Abraham Lincoln; his critics disturbed habitual tabloid thinking.

In spite of all the hard things which may justly be said against tabloid thinking, its service to action is of an importance not to be forgotten. Our enthusiasm for straight thinking must not blind us to the fact that what we do is more important than what we think. We must act effectively, even though we reject tabloid thinking as a method of attaining effective action. So important is action that we can reasonably condemn as crooked thinking any device in thought which has as its purpose the evasion of useful or necessary action. "There is much to be said on both sides, so I shall do nothing about it," is a common type of thinking of those who are too intelligent to fall into the pitfall of popular tabloid thinking, and it is itself a pitfall just as dangerous. Let us call it academic detachment from practical life.

There is, in politics, much to be said for the Republican program, much for the Democratic, and much to be said for a more radical policy. But if we realize this so fully that we do not cast a vote at all, we are doing less than our neighbors who see less clearly than ourselves. Something is going to happen as a result of the poll, and the effect of our abstention from voting is as likely to affect the result in an undesirable way as any of the three possibilities of voting. By not voting, we have not really escaped from the requirement of playing a part in the election; we have only made it impossible that our part will be a useful one.

We cannot escape the necessity for action, and our conviction that there is much to be said on all sides does not absolve us from the necessity for acting vigorously and effectively on the side on which we think the truest and wisest things can be said. If we are driving a motor vehicle across an open space and an obstacle appears in front of us, we can avoid it by going to the left or to the right. The arguments for both may be about equally balanced. We must, however, do either one or the other wholeheartedly without allowing the excellent case for the other side to affect our action at all. If we are content to say that there is much to be said in favor of both sides and drive straight on, we shall break our necks.

The path of wisdom is to act in an effective and wholehearted manner on the side which seems to us, on the whole, to be the best. Realization of all that can be said on the other side should make us tolerant of those opposed to us and ready to revise our courses of action under the influence of new evidence, but it must not be allowed to interfere with the effectiveness of our action in the direction which we have calmly and clear-sightedly chosen. We must steer a middle course between the rock of tabloid thinking and the whirlpool of academic detachment from practical life. Though tabloid thinking is practically useful, it is obviously a hindrance to straight thinking. If truth, and not idleness or convenience is our aim, tabloid thinking is not to be tolerated. Even though tabloid thinking is narrowly useful in providing motives for strenuous action, there is a wider sense in which its results are highly dangerous. Tabloid thinking about our enemies while a war is on may help us to fight effectively, but it is also the continuance of tabloid thinking by Serbs and Bulgars, by Austrians and Italians, by French and Germans, by Russians and the rest of the world, that contains the seeds of the future wars which may produce inconceivable disasters. If the clear thinking which sees both sides of a question made us worse fighters and better keepers of the peace, the world as a whole would be the gainer.

A public man who shows by his speeches that he applies tabloid thinking to international affairs (by, for example, referring to the Government of another nation as a "group of murderers") should be deprived of his office and given an occupation in which tabloid thinking would be more useful. He might, for example, find a congenial field of usefulness as a football cheerleader. Tabloid thinking in affairs inside the nation may be worse. No one can know what horrors of future strife may develop from tabloid thinking about "strikers," "capitalists," "workers," and "agitators."

CHAPTER EIGHT

Pitfalls in Analogy

I N the course of explaining any rather abstract matter, it is an advantage to use an illustration in
order to make one's meaning clear. In an earlier chapter, when describing the evil of allowing our brains to
degenerate into automatic organs, I said that this was
like using a razor for digging the ground. In another
book, when trying to explain that instincts which
have no useful outlet in behavior find one for themselves, I compared this with what happens to a leaky
boiler. Such illustrations are a common and useful device in explanation. A mental picture is easier to understand than a form of words.

These illustrations are merely intended to give a
vivid picture of an abstract matter; they are not
meant to be a method by which we can find out anything new about it. When, on the other hand, we use
a concrete illustration in order to deduce new conclusions, it is no longer a mere illustration, it is an
argument "by analogy."

Let us suppose that after the illustration of the
boiler, I had pointed out that if the steam had no outlet at all the boiler would burst, and had concluded
from this that if human instincts had no outlet in be-

havior a serious mental upheaval would result. Then, if I had no other reason for making this statement than the alleged resemblance between human instincts and steam in a boiler, I should be relying on an argument by analogy. In point of fact, there are other reasons for saying that the damming up of outlets for instinctive behavior leads to mental disorder (actual observations of human life), so the burst boiler can quite properly be used as an illustration. If, however, we had no such observations, the analogy from a boiler would obviously be a very weak and unconvincing reason for concluding that mental disturbance would follow a complete stopping up of instinctive outlets.

The argument by analogy is not necessarily a dishonest or crooked method of thought, although it is a dangerous one always requiring careful examination. Reduced to its bare bones, it can be expressed as the argument that because N has the properties A and B which belong to M, it must also have the property C which too belongs to M. Displayed like this, the argument does not sound a very convincing one. Things which are alike in some respects differ in others. A and B may be respects in which M and N resemble one another, while C may happen to be a property in which M differs from N. A whale resembles a fish in the general shape of its body and in the fact that it lives in water. If we knew no better, an argument from analogy would lead us erroneously to suppose that the whale also resembled a fish in breathing by gills instead of lungs. There is a well-known principle in arguing from analogy that we can only safely argue from the possession of one set of characters to another if there is a causal connection between them. Even this principle would not, however, save us from error here, because the possession of gills is causally connected with the fact of living in water. This just happens to be a character in which whales differ from fishes.

An argument by analogy is not always expanded into a clearly recognizable form. When a writer refers to "the keen edge of an argument" or to "filling the mind of the child with facts," an analogy is implied, in the one case between an argument and a knife or sword, in the other between a mind and a bucket, bag, or box. Such an analogy, implied by the choice of words but not definitely expressed, is a metaphor. A metaphor may be used merely for the purpose of illustration, but if (whether purposely or not) the user of a metaphor draws any new conclusions from the implied analogy, then he is using the argument from analogy although in a somewhat disguised form. Metaphor abounds in all our thinking about abstract matters, and leads to the dangers to straight thinking resulting from unrecognized arguments by analogy.

Against a too drastic condemnation of argument by analogy, it may be urged that analogy underlies a great part of science and that many generally accepted scientific conceptions are really analogies from familiar objects. Thus molecules, atoms, and electrons are thought of and treated as if they were tiny fragments of solid matter; the ether of space as if it were an elastic fluid with peculiar properties; the behavior of falling bodies as if it were due to an attraction by the earth. The startling success with which physics used these conceptions to build up a consistent science and to predict facts which turned out on investigation to be true left men in no doubt that such analogical reasoning was sound at bottom. Indeed, the fact that these conceptions were analogies was very largely forgotten.

Yet, in every one of the three cases I have mentioned, a point was reached at which the analogy broke down. There were properties of electrons which were not conceivably those of lumps of matter, however small; it was found that if all space were filled with an ether it must have the absurd property of both moving and being stationary with respect to the earth at the same time; and certain properties of gravitational fields could not be expressed in terms of invisible elastic threads.

So the most recent physical science turns away from all these concrete representations and expresses observable facts by means of mathematical equations. Thus it becomes entirely incomprehensible for most of us, for we must think in terms drawn from what we can see and handle—that is, by analogies. Such analogies help us very little in comprehending a four-dimensional space-time system and not at all in grasping the latest developments of the quantum theory.

We must not conclude that thinking by analogy has proved itself a thoroughly unsound method of

thought. Our scientific thinking is throughout largely
dependent on analogy and yet has proved an invalu-
able guide to the discovery of new truth. Darwin was
led to his theory of the origin of species largely by
consideration of analogies between the activities of
the breeder and the conditions under which animals
and plants survive in the wild state, and this analogy
is embodied in the term "natural selection." Similarly, the very fruitful conception of "the struggle for
existence" is based on an analogy between these conditions of survival and a physical struggle in which
the stronger kills the weaker. Even when in physics
we have succeeded in transcending the analogies by
which our first steps were guided, this has only been
possible because these analogies guided our thought
about molecules, lines of force, gravitational attraction, etc., along right lines.

The final fate, however, even of these solidly established analogies of physical science re-enforces the
conclusion already suggested: analogies are a valuable guide as to the direction in which to look for
truth, but are never final evidence as to what we
shall discover. We must not forget too that science
has also followed analogies which have misled her
and that the valuable analogies are those which have
been selected because of their power of predicting new
truth. Combustion was at one time attributed to a material called "phlogiston," which was supposed to
leave the burning object. In the same way. Lamarck
was misled by a false analogy when he attributed the
adaptations of organisms to a process resembling that

of the changes which take place in the body when part of it is exercised by use. He supposed that the long neck of the giraffe was due to the cumulative effect of successive generations of giraffes reaching up to high leaves, just as the arm muscle of an individual who habitually lifts heavy weights will increase in girth. A similar misleading analogy in psychology was Mesmer's guess that the phenomena of hypnotism were due to a "nervous effluence" proceeding from the fingertips of the hypnotizer.

The examples we have given of successful analogies in the history of science show how very far a good analogy may prove to be a true guide. A good guide whose reliability is certain to give out somewhere can, however, only be treated in one way by sensible people—with caution. We can never feel certain of a conclusion which rests only on analogy, and we must always look for more direct proof. Also we must examine all our methods of thought carefully, because thinking by analogy is much more extensive than many of us are inclined to suppose.

Analogies also underlie much of our thinking about human beings and their institutions—that is, in psychology and the social sciences. When, for example, we speak of "sick industries," we are thinking of these industries as if they were themselves human beings and not merely the modes of employment of human beings. Such a way of thinking may be partly appropriate, but it may also be partly misleading. When the patriot says, "What matter how I suffer, so long as my country prospers?" he is thinking of his

[108]

country as a kind of superperson. This analogy may lead to the appropriate and admirable behavior of sacrificing himself for the good of his country. Some too-fervent nationalists are led by this analogy, however, into a kind of thinking which may be expressed as: "What matter how I and all my fellow-countrymen suffer so long as our country prospers?" This is obviously pushing the analogy beyond the point at which it ceases to be a reasonable guide to conduct. Common sense demands that one should remember that the prosperity of the country is only a picturesque way of expressing the prosperity of Mr. Brown, Mrs. Brown, and their family, of Mr. Jones, Mrs. Jones, and their family, and of a few million other people, and that unless the happiness of these individuals is secured, there is no reasonable sense in which their country can be said to prosper.

In psychology, too, much of our thinking has been based on physical analogies, and in the past these analogies have proved less trustworthy than the analogies we have mentioned in physics. The way of thinking of the mind as composed of separate "faculties" of memory, imagination, etc., seems to be based on analogy with the arms, legs, etc., which are parts of the body. Careful investigation has shown that many of these "parts" of the mind have no claim to existence at all. The grand theory of "association of ideas" treated ideas as if these were like separable physical things linked by physical bonds. This way of conceiving thought proved serviceable over a certain range of facts, but it breaks down on a closer study of those mental processes in which there are no separable ideas at all.

Our more modern psychological analogies should also be distrusted. "Mental energy" or "libido," for example, is thought of as if it were a stream which, if it is dammed by hindrances to love in adult life, may overflow its earlier channels of our childhood's affections. We may use such an analogy with confidence so far as actual observation of human life gives us reason to believe that it is a reliable guide; we may use it too to suggest new possibilities to be tested afterward by actual observation; but we cannot draw new conclusions from it as to how human beings will behave and suppose that, apart from observation, these will possess any scientific validity.

So far we have been dealing with analogies that are, at any rate, the best available; they do not contain obvious imperfections although they may be of limited reliability as methods of discovering truth. In argument, however, one frequently meets with analogies which are so imperfect that their use must be attributed either to the incompetence or to the dishonesty of the user.

For example, the view that a revival of internal trade was sufficient to restore prosperity has been derided by reference to a dog living by eating its own tail. Let us consider this analogy carefully. If we assume the tail of an animal will go on growing after being bitten off (which is quite possible though not, as it happens, true of a dog), then the case of such an animal eating its own tail does present some analogy with a country living on internal trade. The body-building and energy-supplying elements in the food of the dog correspond to the consumable goods in the country. The argument is intended to prove that the country could not continue to exist without importation of such goods from outside.

On looking more deeply into the argument we see that there are vital differences between the two cases which vitiate the analogy. In the body of a dog there is necessary wastage of its foodstuffs to supply the animal with heat and movement, and no possibility of replacement of this wastage except by taking in food from outside. It is physically impossible for the dog to generate his own proteins and carbohydrates from nothing, so, however generously his tail went on growing, he would be bound to die of starvation in the end if he had nothing but that to eat. The consumable goods of a country differ in this essential respect. Wealth can be generated in a country without taking in anything from outside, and this happens whenever labor is usefully employed. Every time a man sows a grain of corn and reaps an ear, or joins together two or more pieces of material to form a serviceable instrument, he is increasing the country's goods. The point, therefore, at which the dog eating his own tail supports the conclusion of the argument is the very respect in which the analogy is imperfect. What is contended may well be true, but it certainly cannot be proved by this argument.

I have also heard the democratic election of members of Congress attacked on the ground that children are not regarded as capable of electing their own teachers. Again, however, the analogy is obviously imperfect. Adult men and women are presumed to know more about the qualities required of an efficient ruler than children know about those of a good teacher. Moreover, governing and teaching are such very different functions that a method of selection serviceable in the one case may not be in the other. In addition, the democratic selection of the governing class partly serves to secure that those who rule shall not do so in their own interest; no similar problem arises with teachers. In fact there is so little analogy between the selection of teachers and a Congressional election that no conclusions can safely be drawn by analogy from one to the other, whatever other weighty and reasonable objections may be urged against democracy.

Westbrook Pegler often uses the argument by analogy, adapting it to his own ironic style. For instance, because labor unions insist that employers hire separate individuals for separate jobs, Mr. Pegler depicted the plight of a night-club proprietor in "Chez Capone" when a representative of a musician's union objected because the drummer in the band also "socked the brass."

A new man was therefore installed for that purpose, whereupon the drummer was discovered striking the triangle. Again the union representative protested.

[1] "You mean I got to have a whole guy to whang that dinky little triangle a few times a night?" demanded the proprietor. "To hell with it. Wallie, don't whang that gag no more. We will just cut it out of the orchestra."

"You do and we jerk you out of here so fast you trample yourself in the rush," the union representative replied. "You will use a full crew or no crew."

Mr. Pegler described subsequent developments as follows:

"So the agent put a triangle-whanger up on the stand, and things went along all right until the agent heard a couple of those Cuban gourds with the bird-shot in them. It was the drummer in dutch again. His card didn't permit him to shake those gourds, and the agent wouldn't leave until they put on another guy. The orchestra platform was getting crowded, and it was still more crowded when the agent caught the drummer kicking the trap for the big drum, and put in a big drum trap-kicker to do that for him.

"Well, as the night wore on the agent made life more and more miserable for the leader and Mr. Chez Capone. He put on a guy to play hoofbeats with the coconuts, a guy to play the blocks, and another to swish that wire egg-beater thing. He put in another guy to play the sandpaper thing and still another to clank the cowbell—all jobs formerly performed by the drummer in his spare time. He put in

[1] Excerpts reprinted by permission of the *New York World-Telegram, Chicago Daily News* and United Feature Syndicate.

a man to play the boat whistle and another to blow the rubber raspberry gag, and every time the poor drummer would reach for one of his accustomed gags to give it a little sock or twirl or blow, the agent would shove through the Chez Capone, bouncing the customers around to put another hand to work."

It is perhaps unnecessary to point out that no musicians' union actually lays down any such rules as Mr. Pegler describes. But exactly because these rules do not apply to musicians, they seem to represent the settled policy of all union labor. As a result, when Mr. Pegler describes the Chez Capone closing at quarter of one instead of four o'clock and suspending operations entirely as a result of the union's interference, the reader concludes that although this exact situation never did occur, it represents a convincing picture of the logical and inevitable consequence of unionization. Finally, Mr. Pegler's genius as a humorist enables him not only to take liberties with the truth but to entertain the reader in the process.

The worst that can be urged against such arguments as the above is that the analogies are very imperfect—that is, that they break down on examination A still greater degree of imperfection is to be found when there is no analogy at all and an argument is used in the form of an argument from analogy when there is no reason whatever why the same concrete illustration should not have been used in the opposite way. A Victorian bishop, for example, said that virtue grew when watered by war's red rain. He might just as well have said that vice grew when watered by war's red rain, or that virtue died when watered by war's red weed killer. Such an argument has so little logical justification that we may wonder why it is not immediately rejected.

This leads us to a point in psychology commonly neglected in theoretical discussions of analogy. Whatever may be urged against the logical convincingness of an argument by analogy, it remains true that any analogy, good, imperfect, or obviously absurd, tends to produce conviction in the same immediate and unreasonable way as does repeated affirmation or a good slogan. If you make an argument in the form "A is B, just as C is D" (where A and B are abstract or controversial while C and D are concrete and familiar), then your hearers will immediately tend to believe that A is B quite independently of any real analogy between A/B and C/D. If the relationship between C and D can form a picture in the mind, this makes the process of acceptance easier, but I do not think that this is essential. The mere fact that the argument is in the form of an analogy is often enough to force immediate irrational acceptance.

There seems to be no other explanation of the extraordinary extent to which otherwise intelligent people become convinced of highly improbable things because they have heard them supported by an analogy whose unsoundness should be apparent to an imbecile. We hear them say: "Mr. Willoughby Snooks was so helpful and convincing in his address yesterday. He said that right thinking will remove disease from our bodies just as a policeman will remove a burglar from our house. I always used to feel a difficulty about the cure of disease by thought, but I see it quite clearly now."

"But," you may protest, "getting rid of disease by merely thinking about it is not in the least like getting a policeman to put a burglar out of your house. If you must have an analogy, it seems to be more like dealing with a burglar by going to sleep again and dreaming he isn't there." Your protest is obviously right. The speaker has been led to the absurd opinion that physical disease can be cured by mental methods through his (or her) tendency to accept an argument in the form of an analogy, however loose the analogy may be.

This device of commending a statement by bringing forward an argument in the form of an analogy which has no real force is a pretty common one. At election times, thinking in words seems to be very largely replaced by picturesque metaphors and analogies. Flowing tides, harpooned walruses, opponents trimming their sails or casting away their sheet anchors, replace the more prosaic ways of thinking of normal times. No doubt it all aids impassioned conviction, although it may be doubted whether this kind of thinking does much toward solving the real problems of the country.

Typical of this tendency is the speech of a politician who referred to a radical opponent as "sailing as near to the socialist wind as he can without up-

setting his frail craft." [2] The speaker has given no reason beyond mere assertion that his opponent would
be as socialistic as possible, but in a way that carries
much more conviction than the bare verbal statement.
The picture of the radical leader timorously edging
his boat as close to the wind as he dare sticks in the
mind persistently and is accepted readily: if the
speaker had said bluntly what he meant instead of
putting it in the form of an analogy, it is probable
that his hearers would have been less inclined to believe him.

While, therefore, thinking by analogy is not to be
regarded as necessarily crooked thinking, the use of
an imperfect analogy may be a really crooked argument. Much more crooked is the last trick we have
mentioned of using a metaphor or an argument in the
form of analogy when no true analogy exists at all.
Let us call this device a "forced analogy." Although
these two dishonest devices in argument may be re-

[2] To object that sailing too near the wind is not liable to upset
a boat, but only to make it stop, would be to lay one's self open
to a just charge of "diversion by irrelevant objection" (p. 41).
It shows, however, ignorance and incompetence to make such
a slip in an analogy or in a metaphor, for, even if the objection
is not made, it will occur to the minds of many hearers and
interfere with the process of creating belief. Many candidates
in fishing districts have aroused mirth instead of conviction by
inept metaphors of fishing and sailing. Of the same order of
error is the "mixed metaphor" in which different parts of the
picture suggested are inconsistent with one another, such as
the newspaper report of the Allied soldiers "opposed to a
numerical superiority of the cream of the German army tuned
to concert pitch."

garded as different degrees of the same defect, it seems better to treat them as distinct errors, since they are used in a different way and demand different methods of refutation.

Imperfect analogies occur commonly in serious discussion and are best dealt with by simply pointing out where the analogy breaks down. This is, for example, what I did with the argument of the dog eating its own tail.

Forced analogies, on the other hand, are commonly found in the course of public speeches. Their looseness is too obvious to stand against the kind of criticism they would meet in free discussion. They rely for their effect on the readiness of the mind to accept immediately any vivid metaphorical or analogical presentation of a matter. When one finds oneself driven to belief by a well-worded analogy like that of virtue watered by war's red rain, one can begin by examining how close the analogy is. Realizing that it is not at all close, one can try other analogies, as that of vice watered by war's red rain. Finding that these have no less force than the original analogy, the nature of the device used is apparent and its effect in forcing conviction disappears.

CHAPTER NINE

On Drawing the Line

THERE is a venerable law of logic called the "law of excluded middle" which states that A is either B or not B. Thus a piece of paper is either white or not white. This is obviously true, and I shall not deny its soundness as a law of pure logic. At the same time, we must notice that the kind of thinking embodied in this law may be dangerous and misleading when applied to a certain very common range of facts.

Let us begin by considering the case of white paper. The whiteness of paper depends on the amount of light that it reflects to our eyes. We should call the paper on which this book is printed "white" because it reflects a great deal of light and absorbs very little. Yet it does not reflect all. If we coated it with certain chemical substances it would reflect more, but still it would not reflect all the light falling on it. If we coated it very lightly with something that made it reflect less light, we might still call it white. As we increased the depth of the coating, however, we should soon reduce the brightness of the surface so much that we should be compelled to call it a light gray, afterward a dark gray, and finally black. The fact that we call it black, however, would not mean that the surface reflected no light. If we coated it with lamp-black it would reflect still less light, and would, therefore, be even blacker, but it would still be reflecting some of the light that fell on it.

So the division of papers into those that are white and those that are not white is not, in practice, a useful way of dealing with their properties. We shall see later this is true also of more important properties than the whiteness of paper. The trouble lies in the fact that whiteness is a property which papers can have in any quantity, that no paper is 100 per cent white and that there is no real dividing line between papers that have enough of this property to be called white and those that have not. If we arbitrarily make a dividing line and call, let us say, any paper that reflects more than 80 per cent of the light falling on it "white," and any paper reflecting less than this "gray" or "black," we have made a distinction which may be highly misleading, for we may have two white papers (reflecting, let us say 81 per cent and 95 per cent) and one gray paper (reflecting 79 per cent) such that the difference between the gray and one of the whites is far less than the difference between the two whites.

At the same time, we must notice that these facts do not in any way reduce the real difference between a black and a white paper. The white of this page and the black of its print are different qualities although it would be possible to pass from one to the other by a series of imperceptible steps. If a printer orders a roll of white paper from a factory and they send a roll of black paper, and when he complains, they argue that no paper is 100 per cent white and that the paper they sent is not 0 per cent white, and that no exact line can be drawn between papers that are white and those that are not white, the printer will rightly charge them with crooked thinking and refuse to accept the roll. Actually no one would be deceived by such a simple fallacy in connection with white paper, although it is a kind of argument often used in more important matters, as we shall see later. We are not likely to forget that the *degree* of whiteness is an important property of paper.

There is an alternative way of dealing with the whiteness of paper—a way which is, in fact, used in practice. We can think of whiteness as a property arranged along a line which has at one end the property of reflecting 100 per cent of light (pure whiteness) and, at the other end, the property of reflecting 0 per cent light (pure blackness). Between these two extremes we can construct a scale showing all the intermediate percentages of light that can be reflected. Every piece of white, gray, or black paper can be assigned to some position on this scale. We can then say that such a piece of paper reflects 95 per cent of the light falling on it, another reflects 85 per cent, another 65 per cent, another 50 per cent, and another 10 per cent. We have by this method indicated the facts much more precisely than we could by calling the first two papers white, the next two gray, and the last black. At the same time, we shall retain "white," "gray," and "black" as practically convenient words, although we shall know that it is impossible to make them scientifically precise.

It is now necessary to give a name to the peculiarity of whiteness which makes this kind of treatment necessary and which makes it impossible to deal with the subject properly by talking about "white" and "not white." The property is that we can pass from white to its opposite by any number of small imperceptible steps. We could get specimens of paper which possessed any degree of whiteness and arrange them in a row so that no piece of paper ever differed by more than an inappreciable amount from both of its neighbors, and yet so that the row comprised the whole range from the whitest to the blackest paper procurable. Let us call this property, the property of "continuous variation."

All over human life we find properties which show continuous variation, and (just as in the case of white and black) we find this property obscured by the use of words implying sharp distinctions. "Sane" and "insane"; "good" and "bad"; "intelligent" and "unintelligent"; "proletarian" and "capitalist," are pairs of opposites which show this property of continuous variation. Our use of the two sharply contrasted terms "sane" of ourselves and our neighbors, and "insane" of the unfortunate persons confined in mental hospitals, leads us to forget the continuity between them. The essential difference between the sane and insane is, however, simply the degree to which they are able to adapt themselves to their environments. This power of successful adaptation varies quite continuously from one individual to another; no one has it perfectly and probably no one has quite lost it. We could make a continuous row of people progressively less well adapted, with the sanest of ourselves at one end and the most insane inhabitants of mental hospitals at the other. Any argument, therefore, which begins in some such way as follows: "A man must be either sane or insane, and an insane person is absolutely incapable of reasonable thought . . ." is a dangerous piece of crooked thinking, since it ignores this fact of continuity.

This kind of thinking crops up constantly in political controversies, especially in the utterances of extremists of every type. To Communists, Fascists, and Nazis the world is always at an historic turning point and a clear-cut decision must be made one way or another—and instantly. R. Palme Dutt, the foremost Communist pamphleteer writing the English language, has posed the problem of capitalism versus socialism almost every month for the past fifteen years in the *Labour Monthly*. In October, 1931, for example, just after the formation of the first National Government of Great Britain, he led off his "Notes of the Month" as follows:

"The fight is here—the fight of which revolutionary Marxism has given consistent warning as inevitably developing from the present stage of crisis of British capitalism. Every other issue is torn aside by the ever deepening reality of the crisis of capitalism, and the consequent sharpening of class struggle. The great 'Either—Or,' the fight for existence of the bourgeoisie and working class in the death agonies of British capitalism, advances to a new and grimmer stage. . . .

"The crisis marches on relentlessly, caring neither for Labour Government nor National Government, working out the laws of capitalism in all their anarchy and barbarism. Unrest rises throughout the working class, through the armed forces of the state, through the professional workers and lower middle class, through all strata of the population other than the big bourgeoisie and their hangers-on. What a demonstration of the truth of the revolutionary line of the growing instability of capitalism and the revolutionization of the working class, which but two years ago was still doubted and denied and scoffed at even by many would-be Marxists, who saw only stabilization and depression. Great issues, great struggles, are before us."

This fatalistic definition of black and white issues is not peculiar to the Communist press. Fascists and Nazis express themselves just as positively. And representatives of middle-of-the-road bourgeois liberalism take them at their word. Hamilton Fish Armstrong used a phrase of Mussolini's as the title for his booklet, *We Or They?* and quoted this statement from which the phrase was drawn: "The struggle between two worlds can permit of no compromise. . . . Either we or they! Either their ideals or ours! Either our state or theirs!"

Writing on Fascism in the *Enciclopedia Italiana*,

Mussolini resorted to the same device in defining the attitude of Fascism toward peace and war: "It (Fascism) thus repudiates the doctrine of pacifism—born of a renunciation of the struggle and an act of cowardice in the face of sacrifice. War alone brings up to its highest tension all human energy and puts the stamp of nobility upon the people who have the courage to meet it. All other trials are substitutes that never really put men into the position where they have to make the great decision—the alternative of life or death."

Adolf Hitler placed an even sharper alternative before the German people when he said, shortly after taking office: "Let the parties of destruction know this one thing: that as long as the Almighty gives me life, my desire and my determination to destroy them will remain boundless. Never shall I be ready for compromise. Of Marxism and the German people, only one can triumph, and it is Germany that will win."

Before he assumed office Hitler expanded on the same theme at greater length: "If the National Socialist movement that we have created as a counterweight to Marxism were to collapse today, Germany would go Bolshevik tomorrow. Destiny itself will draw a clear line of battle. We are seeing fulfilled among our own people the Biblical text that recognizes hot or cold but that damns lukewarmness to destruction. The middle group is being hewed and hacked to pieces. The period of compromise is approaching its end. Today the German nation confronts

[125]

international Bolshevism with National Socialism."

Intelligence has been mentioned as one of the examples of continuous variation being obscured in ordinary thinking. When we use such words as "idiot," "imbecile," "backward," "normal," "bright," "genius," we are inclined to think of people as divided by their inborn gifts into really distinct classes. Measurement of intelligence by intelligence tests shows that this is not the case. If we take a thousand children and measure their intelligence by testing we shall find that every degree of intelligence from about 30 per cent to 170 per cent of the normal is represented among them, that the commonest values are the central ones (about normal), while there are fewer of the extremely high and the extremely low values. But there are no natural dividing lines between the different classes "idiot," "imbecile," etc.; in making these distinctions we are drawing lines where none exist in fact. This is often a practically convenient thing to do, but if it misleads us into thinking that the real difference between "backward" and "normal" children is as sharp as the difference between the words we use, we have been led into crooked thinking. The error here lies in the fact that by using separate words to distinguish two extremes showing continuous variation between them, we are making a sharp distinction appear where there is none in fact. A great deal of our thinking has to be revised if we are to recognize the continuity between sanity and insanity, between intelligence and unintelligence, between goodness and badness, between religion and irreligion, between civilization and uncivilization, and between different social classes. The difficulty is one recognized in popular speech as the difficulty of knowing "where to draw the line." Where no sharp distinctions exist in fact, the use of sharply different words to distinguish facts which show continuous variation only distorts the realities we are trying to describe.

This is the first kind of crooked thinking into which we may be led when dealing with facts showing continuous variation—that we may make sharp distinctions in speech where none exists in fact. There is another which is the opposite of this: we may deny the reality of differences because there is continuous variation between the different things. A very old example illustrates this error. One may throw doubt on the reality of a beard by a process beginning by asking whether a man with one hair on his chin has a beard. The answer is clearly "No." Then one may ask whether with two hairs on his chin a man has a beard. Again the answer must be "No." So again with "three," "four," etc. At no point can our opponent say "Yes," for if he has answered "No" for, let us say, twenty-nine hairs, and "Yes" for thirty, it is easy to pour scorn on the suggestion that the difference between twenty-nine and thirty hairs is the difference between not having and having a beard. Yet by this process of adding one hair at a time we can reach a number of hairs which would undoubtedly make up a beard. The trouble lies in the fact that the difference between a beard and no beard is like the difference

[127]

between white and gray in the fact that one can pass by continuous steps from one to the other.

In this argument, the fact of continuous variation has been used to undermine the reality of the difference. Because there is no sharp dividing line, it has been suggested that there is no difference. This is clearly a piece of crooked argument which would take in no reasonable person, so long, at any rate, as it was used about beards and not about anything which engaged our emotions more strongly.

A similar error lay at the back of the mind of the man who loaded his camel one straw at a time, hoping that the additional weight of a single straw would never be enough to injure the camel. When at length the camel's back broke, he attributed it to the extra weight of the last straw. He supposed that because there was no sharp line between a moderate load and a severe overload, there was, therefore, no difference between them. Again this is a mistake which no reasonable person would make.

We do, however, frequently hear an argument against the distinction between a proletarian and a capitalist which begins: "When does a man become a capitalist? If a working man has $100 in the bank, is he a capitalist?" This is the argument of the beard. Those who would not be deceived in connection with beards, readily swallow the same piece of crooked thinking when it is used in connection with matters on which their emotions are stronger. The truth is, of course, that the difference between those who own capital and those who do not is one of the most important of the external differences between men, although there is continuous variation between those who own nothing and those who own a great deal. It is equally wrong to suppose that there is a sharp dividing line between these classes and to suppose that there is no difference between them. The justification for using the terms "capitalist" and "proletarian" (or "bourgeois" and "proletarian") in social thinking is the same as the justification for using the words "white" and "black," and their use is open to the same dangers.

These difficulties concerning continuous variation are by no means of merely academic interest. The difficulty of knowing where to "draw the line" is so universal in the kind of matter with which modern thought is engaged that many of our traditional methods of thinking which suppose that we are dealing with things entirely separate from one another fail us altogether.

Once we thoroughly realize this fact, an old method of insuring straight thinking—by defining one's terms and by insisting on one's opponent doing so too—becomes very difficult to us. A good definition makes an idea precise and sharply distinguished from other ideas. But clearly this may be no help but a grave hindrance if it marks off sharply in our thought things which are not sharply marked off in fact.

So this device of badgering one's opponent to define his terms may really be a piece of crooked argumentation. It may be an attempt to make him provide clear-cut ideas with which the other person can play

[129]

an intellectual game (as with counters) which has little relationship with the realities which are under discussion. It has been said, with some truth, that we can judge how modern is a book on psychology or sociology by the fewness of its definitions.

Defining a term means giving the general properties of what is described, together with the particular property which distinguishes it from all other members of the same class. Its definition is a formula which cuts it off and isolates it from all other things. Thus an even number can be defined as a finite integer divisible by two, and the old definition of man was that man was a rational animal. It is, in fact, perfectly sound and useful to define an even number, a straight line, or a triangle, for these are sharply distinct things. There is no sort of finite integer intermediate between an odd and an even number.

You cannot, on the other hand, usefully define a white object or an intelligent child, for there is, as we have seen, continuity between whiteness and blackness and between intelligence and unintelligence. The definition of man as a rational animal is of little usefulness in practice, because rationality is a thing which shows continuous variation. Some men show much less than others, and a human child of two has less rationality than an average fully developed chimpanzee. It is true that mankind as existing now does form a distinct class not grading by continuous steps into the other animals. But an indefinitely large number of steps must have so connected him in the past; the fossil remains of Pithecanthropus and Sinanthropus show some of these intermediate steps. The evolution of man from lower animals is true in fact, but can easily be made to appear absurd by a speculative argument based on a definition of man as a rational animal.

The worst danger of all in too great reliance on definitions is that one may be creating conceptions by definition which correspond to nothing whatever in fact. It is as easy to define unicorn as to define rhinoceros. Such definition may lead us into the danger that, when we suppose we are talking about realities, we may only be talking about ideas that have been constructed by our definitions and which correspond to nothing outside.

This is a danger always present in abstract thinking. We can create a consistent theory of psychology by defining will, memory, attention, etc., but we have no guarantee that what we have defined are the names of anything which has a separate existence in fact. We may be playing a delightful and intricate intellectual game which has nothing whatever to do with the true subject matter of psychology—what actual people think and do. We may all the time be talking about unicorns and not rhinoceroses. In the same way, we can define value in an economic discussion without being sure that any precise set of facts is indicated by the word we have defined.

CHAPTER TEN

Vagueness and Related Evils

DEFINITION was intended as a safeguard against all the crookedness in thought which results from either the speaker or the listener in a discussion being uncertain as to the exact meaning with which words are being used, or from a similar uncertainty existing (as it well may) in the mind of an individual thinker even when he is not engaged in discussion with anyone else. However convinced we may be that the reckless use of definition has its own dangers, we must still concern ourselves with freeing thought and discussion from these perils. Vagueness in thought and speech is not to be tolerated. Used in moderation and in conjunction with other methods of making thought clear, the method of definition will be found to be a valuable weapon in the overcoming of vagueness.

The most useful kind of definition will, it is true, not generally be the formal definition of the textbooks of logic. When the things we are talking about are not sharply distinguished in fact from related things, we cannot usefully or properly try to cut them off sharply in thought. To devise a definition of "religion," for example, which would satisfy textbook requirements would be a waste of ingenuity. But that does not excuse us from the necessity of being prepared to say as clearly and as precisely as we can what we mean by the word.

The most obvious piece of crooked thinking which results from an absence of clear meanings is that in which a word is used in different senses in different parts of the same argument. A popular writer on "crowd psychology," for example, begins by pointing out the cruelty, irresponsibility, and lack of intelligence of a crowd (that is, of an actual gathering in street or market place of people with a common interest). He then points out that cruelty, irresponsibility, and lack of intelligence are necessary faults of democratic government, because democracy is governed by the crowd. Here, however, he has obviously changed the meaning of the word "crowd," using it first in its literal sense and secondly in a vague metaphorical sense.

Similarly, in popular discussion of industrial relationships, the terms "labor" and "capital" are used both with their strict economic meaning of work and accumulated wealth, and also as meaning "worker" and "capitalist" (which is, for example, the meaning implied in the common conclusion that "capital and labor are complementary to one another"). The meanings of the terms may shift from one to the other of these in the course of a single argument so that the words are used in one sense in the premises and in the other in the conclusion.

This habit of using words with two meanings not

distinguished is "ambiguity." [Bad as this fault is, it is only a minor degree of vagueness. If a word is used with no particular meaning or meanings but only with a general tendency in some direction, we have a more extreme form of the disease which makes accurate thought and reasonable discussion impossible]

In order to be vague it is not necessary that a statement should also be obscure. It often is, and more or less deliberate obscurity is often a cloak for vagueness. But the simplest statement or thought may be vague if it does not embody a clear meaning in the mind of the person making it. This is particularly liable to happen with abstract words. Such words, for example, as "principle," "wealth," "mind," "spiritual" have meanings which can never be carried by a mental image of an outside object or action or of a relation between outside objects or actions. Their proper meaning is a kind of summary or abstraction of many different outside things.

We all of us hear many such words which at the beginning carry no meaning for us at all, and we are quite likely to take them over into our vocabulary before they have a clear meaning. To obtain clear meanings for any but the common names of outside things requires a certain amount of mental effort, and idleness leads us to be content with taking many words into our speech and thought without making this mental effort.

Let us first consider how to get rid of vagueness from our own minds before we consider how we can combat our opponent's vagueness in argument. We can begin by consulting definitions. Habitual recourse to the dictionary whenever we meet with a new word before taking it into our vocabulary is a useful rule which helps against the development of words without clear meanings in our vocabularies.

While the use of dictionary definition should save us from using words with shifting and variable meanings, it does not do everything that is necessary to make them a serviceable part of our mental equipment for straight thinking. In order to provide an example of the further difficulties which must be overcome, let us consider a fairly new technical word in medical psychology which has escaped into popular speech, where it is misused as badly as is possible. This is the word "complex."

Let us turn to a definition of this word and see whether it provides us with complete safeguards against its improper use. We shall not find it in dictionaries, but in the glossary of a recent psychological textbook I find a definition which I have slightly shortened as follows: "COMPLEX: A group of ideas linked together because they form a chain in some potential instinctive reaction. A complex is always unconscious or, at least, owes its importance to elements in it which remain unconscious."

If we understand all parts of this definition and the rather unusual sense in which the author is using the words "idea" and "unconscious," we should have a fairly clear notion of the way to describe a complex, and we should be certain that a number of ways of using the word were not what is intended by the definition. We should not, however, have any confidence that we knew how to use the word in practice or what kinds of facts in human nature ought to be labeled by it, any more than from having read an accurate description in words of a deep-sea fish, we should be able to draw the fish or even to recognize it if we saw it.

We may thus know in words what "complex" means and yet find that it does not for us serve the purpose of indicating anything whatever. For us it remains, in a sense, meaningless. Probably the vocabulary of most people contains some words which are thus meaningless. Even if they can say in other words what they mean, they cannot make use of them in understanding the external facts they are meant to deal with. Any mental activity they carry out by means of such words hardly deserves the name of thinking. It is rather a kind of mental game carried out with word habits. The game may amuse the player, but it cannot guide him to sound conclusions which he can apply to the world outside him.

Something more must be done after we have read and mastered the definition of "complex." We must ask also for an example or examples of what is meant. Let us suppose that someone who undertakes to explain the word to us goes on to describe the mental origins of the so-called "nervous" disorders, such as a long-forgotten fright in childhood from an oncoming train producing in later life a persistent terror of going more than a few hundred yards from home,

[136]

or forgotten childish resentment against one's father producing a later passionate hatred of kings, judges, policemen, and all in authority. After having heard these illustrations, we may be able to say: "Now I see what you mean by 'complex.'"

The word "complex" now arouses in our minds ideas of the sources of peculiarities in emotion and behavior which we have actually experienced. It has a usable meaning. The definition alone may have connected it up with nothing but a set of other words which in combination had no clear meaning for us.

Of course the two examples of complexes given are by themselves not a sufficient system of ideas to have attached to the word to make it a serviceable part of our mental equipment. Under their guidance, however, we should soon gain enough experience of our own and other people's complexes to enrich the system of ideas connected with the word; the definition also playing a useful part in this process by enabling us to decide which of the curious phenomena of behavior we are to attribute to complexes and which not. So, by the combined use of the method of definition and the method of illustration, we have gained a clear and useful meaning to the word and are saved from the danger of using it vaguely and also from the danger of using it without reference to anything real in the world around us.

It is a good plan in the course of reading, talking, or even merely thinking in abstract terms to keep our thought closely in contact with earth by continually challenging ourselves to give particular examples as illustrations of general statements. Otherwise our abstract terms may be so devoid of meaning to us (whatever they may have been to their original users) that our thought has no touch with realities.

We read, for example, in a book on psychology: "The sociological value of instinct transformation lies in the fact that it can provide a socially harmless outlet for otherwise objectionable behavior tendencies." We pause and think, "It is a good thing for Tommy to play football, because he is then less likely to make a nuisance of himself by fighting other boys or by throwing stones at street lamps." That is one example of what the passage means, so we can be sure that we are not altogether failing to follow the author's meaning. We need not for the moment also stop to think of all the other things it means: the value of writing poetry to Shelley, of tournaments to King Arthur's knights, of keeping cats to those who are lonely, and a great deal more.

We read on, and again come to a passage where we are led to pause to be certain that we have understood: "Deprivation of the nutritive instinct is destructive of the higher cultural interests." We reflect that a man who hasn't enough to eat does not bother about poetry or pictures.

We turn to another book and are held up by the passage: "Pain and pleasant sensation give us the instinct mentality, the content of feeling functions dynamically, as the entity of Instinct action." We try to think of a particular thing that this could mean. The first four words present no difficulty, but afterward we are baffled. We do not understand it, and can make no use of it in our thought. We go back to earlier explanations of the technical terms used; we may even read the whole of the book over without understanding it, in the hope that it will become clear on a second or third reading. If still no particular things seem to us to illustrate the passage we must reluctantly conclude that we do not understand it. This may be the author's fault or our own.

We must not, of course, make the mistake of supposing that a single simple illustration exhausts the meaning of an abstract passage. The abstract terminology is a shorthand way of expressing a large collection of particular facts. Success in abstract thinking means that we really can think of the whole class in its common features and not only of the particular members of it which we may have chosen for illustration. Until we can do this we have not advanced to the level of abstract thought at all. Inability to think in abstract terms is a difficulty which we all have to overcome during the course of our lives, and it is probably a difficulty which is particularly great to those who habitually think in pictures.

When we have reached the level of abstract thinking, however, there appears the further danger which we are at present discussing, that our thought may lose sight altogether of the particular instances which together give the abstract thought its meaning. From this danger it is probable that the person who thinks in pictures is relatively free. It is to avoid this danger that we must be prepared while we are reading to

[139]

challenge ourselves to give an illustration or illustrations in order to guarantee to ourselves that an author's abstract terms are conveying a meaning to us. Similarly, the fact that we can give even a single illustration of any abstract matters we are talking about ourselves is a guarantee that we are not using words without a meaning. Our thought remains in contact with concrete reality.

It is true that there are regions of thought where thought is not in contact with concrete reality and in which the inability of a speaker to give concrete illustrations is no proof that what he says is meaningless. This is true, for example, of some parts of philosophy and of pure mathematics. A man expounding Hegelian philosophy or the theory of infinite numbers will talk very abstractly and will not be able to make his meaning plain by giving concrete illustrations of what he means. There is none possible; but what such a speaker says may not be meaningless.

There are, therefore, regions of thought in which one may not be in contact with concrete reality (that is, with chairs, tables, human beings, and the things human beings do) and yet where thought is not meaningless. This, however, is of no practical importance to us, because ninety-nine per cent of the thought with which we are practically concerned is not in that region. Our concern in psychology is with the thoughts and behavior of concrete human beings; in economics with work and money and the concrete things which are exchanged for money. In these regions, any abstract thinking must be defended from the charge of

[140]

meaninglessness by showing that it means some particular thing or things in concrete fact. It is fair to challenge our opponents to bring forward concrete illustrations to show that their abstract thought is not meaningless, and it is necessary that we should be prepared ourselves to give similar illustrations. Without such precautions our talk will sound very learned, but it will only be a show for fools and not a guide to truth.

The fact that the practical thinking with which we are most concerned is about concrete things imposes other limitations on our thought which we are sometimes inclined to forget. It means, for example, that, in order to arrive at the truth, we are dependent on an adequate supply of facts and not only on accurate methods of thought. It means too that purely speculative thinking apart from facts is of no value in this field as a guide to truth. Hence the insistence of modern science on the necessity for collection of facts by adequate methods of experiment and observation and their sifting and interpretation by adequate mathematical methods.

Unhappily in many of the practical questions which we are called upon to decide, an accurate and complete knowledge of the facts concerned is very difficult to get. So, by the combined effort of mental idleness and the domination of our thought by practical necessities, we are tempted to form final judgments without the necessary basis of fact. We may even be tempted to suppose that accurate thinking without the necessary facts will itself supply our needs.

[141]

Such "speculative thinking" has a certain legitimate use. By speculative thinking alone, man could have found out all the truths of pure mathematics. He could have discovered, for example, that 2 is the cube root of 8 and that 13 is a prime number. He could not, however, by mere speculation have advanced one step in any of the sciences. He could not have found out anything about human nature until he turned to the collection of facts about mankind, or about economics until he began to collect facts about such things as the production and distribution of goods.

The belief that one can find out something about real things by speculation alone is one of the most long-lived delusions in human thought. It is the spirit of antiscience which is always trying to lead men away from the study of reality to the spinning of fanciful theories out of their own minds. It is the spirit which every one of us (whether he is engaged in scientific investigation or in deciding how to use his vote in an election) must cast out of his own mind. Mastery of the art of thought is only the beginning of the task of understanding reality. Without the correct facts it can only lead us into error.

We can distinguish as a special kind of crooked thinking the attempt to get knowledge of fact by speculative methods. This attempt is being made in any argument which tries to deduce what "is" from what the speaker feels "ought to be" or "must be," or whenever a person in discussion tries to draw conclusions about facts from the use of words. Speculation has a legitimate place even in thought about external fact—that of suggesting new possibilities) We have taken the development of non-Euclidean geometries as an example of the legitimate and valuable use of speculation. We can properly use the speculative method to suggest what might be, but never to conclude what is. We can only draw conclusions as to facts by consideration of other facts.

Yet the illegitimate use of speculation is common. Our remedy is to examine on what grounds a conclusion as to fact is put forward. If these grounds are other facts, then the conclusion may or may not be a sound one. If the grounds are the speaker's conviction of what ought to be or what must be or the manner in which words are commonly used, then the conclusion cannot be legitimate, and we must defeat our opponent's argument by showing that his conclusion is based on the kind of data from which no valid conclusion can be drawn.

While speculative thinking is by no means absent from discussions of practical affairs, it is particularly in those dealing with questions of a semiphilosophical order that this trick is prevalent. "Man cannot have evolved from monkeys because the higher cannot be derived from the lower"; "A vacuum cannot be produced because a space not occupied by matter is a contradiction in terms"; "The brain cannot be a mechanism because we cannot conceive how any mechanism, however complicated, could think, de-

[143]

cide, judge," etc. These are all speculative arguments. Some of their conclusions are probably true and some false, but none can be safely asserted on the grounds given.

It may be objected, however, that what is contradictory or inconceivable cannot be true. That is so, but the fact remains that neither principle is in itself of any practical use for discovering truth (that is, the truth with which we are practically concerned in the world around us as distinct from the truths of pure logic and pure mathematics). Decision that things were false because they were inconceivable was at one time regarded as a legitimate method in scientific thinking, but the course of modern science has shown that this criterion is worthless in practice. Its defect is that our inability to conceive of anything may simply be due to the limitations of our thought habits and not to its real impossibility. Non-Euclidean space is entirely inconceivable to most people, yet it apparently exists wherever there is a gravitational field. Many early philosophers were unable to conceive a vacuum, yet experiment showed that it was possible to empty a glass vessel of its air. Some of the most acute critics of generally accepted conceptions found motion inconceivable, yet they and other people managed to walk about.

The position as to contradictoriness as a criterion of truth is less easy. If two statements contradict one another, then one or both of them must be wrong. That is a truth which we cannot afford to ignore in any attempt at straight thinking, and nothing can excuse the common habit of holding two contradictory opinions both as certain.

The practical difficulty lies in the fact that the contradiction may not mean that the two sets of facts we are trying to express are inconsistent with one another, but simply that we are expressing them wrongly. We cannot even conclude from the fact that a statement or theory is self-contradictory that the facts it is trying to express do not exist. It may only be that they are badly expressed.

It is sometimes urged, for example, that there is no unconscious mind because that means an unconscious consciousness, which is self-contradictory. Now, what the theory of the unconscious mind is trying to express is a whole range of facts, of which one sample is that as a result of having in one's childhood been frightened by a dog in a dark passage, one may in later life develop a morbid terror of inclosed spaces although one has never again been aware of the original incident. The above argument about the self-contradictoriness of the unconscious mind is often used as if it demolished the above range of facts. This is an illegitimate use of a speculative argument.

Whether the range of facts that the theory of the unconscious mind is trying to express really exists or not can be settled in one way only—by observation and experiment on human thought and behavior. I believe it does exist. If the theory of the unconscious mind is self-contradictory (which I do not think it is), that can only mean that the facts have been badly expressed in the theory. We must express them in some other way. The self-contradictoriness of the theory can, in itself, decide nothing as to the facts it is trying to express.

On the other hand, it is perfectly legitimate to attack a theory on the ground that it is self-contradictory in order that we may replace the theory by one that is not self-contradictory but which equally well saves the facts. Such a self-consistent theory is likely indeed to be a better guide to the discovery of new truth. But no pedantic preference for tidy theories must make us willing to jettison discovered fact. It is better to hold tentatively a bad theory which is serviceable in practice than to ignore facts in order that we may have a neat and self-consistent theory. It is better to find one's way over the ground by a rough sketch which is an adequate guide than to have a beautiful map which is self-consistent but which does not truly represent the features of the ground.

No method of purely speculative thought can tell us anything about facts of the real world (by which I mean thoughts and feelings as well as chairs and tables). To find out about those facts we must investigate the facts themselves. Having got them, we must think about them as logically as we can. God forbid that anything said in condemnation of the improper use of speculation should be made an excuse for sloppy thinking!

CHAPTER ELEVEN

Prejudice

WE have now discussed several of the ways in which we can think crookedly and in which our tendency to do so can be exploited by unscrupulous propagandists. We must not, however, make the mistake of supposing that mere knowledge of these ways in itself saves us from the danger of wrong thinking. Even if we went much more thoroughly into the matter and bought a first-class textbook of logic, mastered all the forms of the syllogism, and understood all the possible kinds of fallacy, we still could not expect to be freed from error and to be made correct in all our opinions.

We tend to think wrongly not so much because we do not know the laws of logic as because there are obstacles in our own minds which make us unwilling to think straight on certain subjects. These are our "prejudices." The uneducated man who has never heard of the laws of logic may come to quite correct conclusions on such a question, let us say, as the relative chances of drawing a red and a black card by a chance draw from a complete pack, where the facts are simple and the reasoning perfectly straightforward. On the other hand, the learned author of a standard textbook on logic may be quite unable to come to correct conclusions on a question in which his own interests are deeply involved, such a question, for example, as the economic justification of a kind of taxation which bears specially hardly on himself.

Education does not in itself save us from this disability. It ought to help us in the direction of freedom from prejudice, but it does not necessarily do so. Learned men are often as bound by their prejudices as anyone else. The learned man may defend his most unreasonable prejudices by arguments in correct logical form while the uneducated man defends his by illogical arguments. The difference is plainly not much to the advantage of the learned man. The fact that he can marshal formally correct arguments in defense of his errors may make these more watertight against opposing arguments and against opposing experience. His mastery of the art of thought may simply make his unreasonable opinions more unassailable.

Of course, you, being free from his prejudices, may see where the flaw lies in his reasons for holding the opinions, but this flaw may very well not be in the form of his arguments. It may lie in what he assumes, or in what facts he selects of all possible facts to consider. I do not wish to suggest that correct thinking on correct facts can lead to error, but only that there are other routes to error than lack of logic, and the most logical mind guided by its prejudices can and will find its way to error by one of these other routes.

There was an old opinion (still commonly current) that the lunatic is a person suffering from a defect in his power of reasoning. Now no general statement about lunatics is likely to be true, for the term "lunacy" covers some dozen mental disorders all with entirely different characters. The kind of lunatic that people who make this statement had in mind was the kind who believed some absurd proposition, such as that they were reincarnations of some long-dead monarch or that all other persons were engaged in a conspiracy against them—those who suffered from what we call "delusions."

Now if we ever engage in discussion with a gentleman who believes that he is a reincarnation of Napoleon, of Julius Caesar, or of Jesus Christ, we do not find a loss of reasoning power. On the contrary, he reasons most persistently about the very subject of his delusions, and the quality of his reasoning is determinded by his intellectual development. If he has a keen, logical intellect he will reason keenly and logically. He will apply the same standard of reasoning in defense of his delusions as he would, if he were sane, apply to the defense of his sane opinions. This standard may be high. It may also be low. Remember that most sane persons have a pretty low standard of reasoning. Ask the average man in the street why he believes that the world is round and he will give you a set of very bad reasons. Ask the flat-earth fanatic why he thinks the world is flat and he will probably give you a much better set, for his reasoning powers have been sharpened in continual controversy with people holding the orthodox view. Yet he is wrong and the illogical man in the street is right. The man with wrong opinions is not necessarily the worse reasoner.

In the same way, the person suffering from insane delusions may show no loss of reasoning power. His defect is that the opinions he holds are very badly wrong; and that his reasoning is used to support these wrong opinions and not to criticize them. Their source is not reasonable. They form a kind of superprejudice.

When any of us holds the kind of opinions we have called "prejudices," we have a part of our minds in the same condition as that of the delusional system of the insane. We too reason to the best of our ability in defense of our prejudices, but these reasonings are not the real support for our opinions. These are based on other (often quite irrational) grounds.

If we argue directly against the false beliefs of a person suffering from delusional insanity, we shall find our arguments unable to shake his beliefs because they are not directed against the real causes of those beliefs. The more successful of our arguments will, however, have a result dangerous to ourselves, for they may produce an explosion of violent anger. The deep-seated system of emotions protected so carefully by the set of false beliefs will also be protected by anger and physical violence if the protective system of beliefs is in any way threatened.

The same is true to a lesser degree of the opinions of a sane person grounded on emotional or practical needs. He will not willingly allow those beliefs so necessary to his mental comfort to be overthrown, and if our arguments begin to threaten them he will

[150]

grow angry or at least peevish. When he begins to show anger instead of reasonable opposition to our arguments, we may press home our advantage, for this is an indication that his beliefs are beginning to be threatened by our arguments.

This use of an opponent's signs of anger as an indication that we have touched what he feels to be a weak spot in his argument is, of course, a perfectly legitimate device in argument. There is also a dishonest trick which may be used in connection with the anger of an opponent. This is the trick of deliberately angering him in order that we may take advantage of the fact that he will argue less efficiently in a condition of anger. This we may do, not only by pressing on a weak point in his argument, but also by adopting a deliberately offensive or insolent manner, by making fun of matters on which he obviously feels strongly, or by the use of such irritating tricks as diversion by irrelevant objection.

When H. L. Mencken and George Jean Nathan were in their heyday in the early 1920's, they brought the art of vituperation to the highest point it has reached in the United States in recent years. Take this description of the Methodist clergy from the introduction to *The American Credo* published in 1920:

"What one observes is a horde of uneducated and inflammatory dunderheads, eager for power, intolerant of opposition, and full of a childish vanity—a mob of holy clerks but little raised, in intelligence and dignity, above the forlorn half-wits whose souls they chronically rack. In the whole United States there is

[151]

scarcely one among them who stands forth as a man of sense and information. Illiterate in all save elementals, untouched by the larger currents of thought, drunk with their power over dolts, crazed by their immunity to challenge by their betters, they carry into the professional class of the country the spirit of the most stupid peasantry, and degrade religion to the estate of an idiotic phobia. There is not a village in America in which some such preposterous jackass is not in eruption."

Knowledge of the nature of this trick and of its purpose makes the remedy obvious. We must always be determined that nothing shall make us angry in discussion, because, however annoying our opponent may be, we shall best defeat him by keeping our temper under control. If we feel anger arising, this should be a signal to be increasingly courteous to our opponent and increasingly critical of our own position. We can use the first stirrings of anger to detect the weaknesses of our own position as well as can our opponent.

We must examine a little more closely the psychological nature of these things we have called prejudices. To some objects, pleasurable emotions are attached, and we desire these objects and tend to believe any proposition whose truth would secure them. To other objects, unpleasurable emotions are attached, and we turn from these objects and tend to believe any proposition which denies their reality. More simply we may say that we tend to believe what we desire or need to be true and to disbelieve what we desire or need to be false. If we have bet our last dollar on a horse running at a hundred to one, we fervently believe that he will win and we shall hotly contest a friend's proposition that he cannot run and will most likely come in last. Similarly, if a man is suffering from a dangerous illness he tends to refuse to believe that his illness can really be fatal.

We may ask how the emotions which determine our acceptance of some propositions and rejection of others came into existence. Sometimes their origin is obvious. Practically all men desire money and comfort, and fear ruin and death, so they will tend to accept propositions whose truth would secure their wealth, comfort, and security of living, and reject those whose truth would threaten them. We can see how general this law is when we notice how nearly universal is the rule that those who have possessions (even a few) are politically on the side of preservation of the existing order, while revolutionaries are, on the whole, recruited from the nonpossessors.

Sometimes, however, the connection between emotions and prejudices is more obscure. Sometimes the emotion lying behind a prejudice may be a relic of the emotional life of early childhood. Our childish love for our father or our resentment against his discipline may be the determining cause of our adult reverence for authority or of our rebellion against it. Whichever of these two factors was the stronger in our childhood may thus determine whether we shall be monarchists or republicans, conservatives or revolutionaries. Similarly, our sympathy with oppressed peoples may be based on our childhood's phantasies of rescuing our mother from distress. In any case, the connection between the emotion and the resulting opinion is never apparent to the holder of a prejudice. It is of the essential nature of a prejudice that the connection should not be apparent. The prejudiced person believes that he holds his opinion on entirely rational grounds. The deeper the emotional reason for holding his opinion is hidden from the mind of the man with a prejudice, the more strongly is the prejudice held.

Let us suppose that two men are arguing about a proposal for increased surtax on incomes of more than $10,000. One of them is in favor of the new tax. He argues the case in its favor entirely on general grounds, with logical arguments as to its general economic effects. His opponent argues hotly against it with equally general arguments. Neither of them argues the question from any consideration of how the proposal would affect him personally, and both would indignantly repudiate the suggestion that the effect of the tax on themselves plays any part in determining their opinions about it. Yet, as onlookers, we are not surprised to learn that the man arguing for the tax has a smaller, while the man arguing against it has a larger income than $10,000. Nor are we likely to be wrong in guessing that these facts are much more important influences in determining the opinions of the two men than any of the logical arguments they bring forward so impressively.

We must not, however, make the mistake of supposing that, when opinions based quite irrationally on people's personal desires or repugnances are bolstered up by apparently reasonable arguments, this is simply hypocrisy in the ordinary sense. The holder of such an opinion is generally quite unconscious of the irrational grounds of his belief and honestly believes that his reasonable arguments are the real ground for his belief. The true reasons for his belief are hidden from his consciousness. He is not a hypocrite, he is merely a self-deceiver.

Such a rational bolstering up of a belief held on irrational grounds has been called a "rationalization." When our desires lead us to accept a belief, our minds construct an apparently rational set of reasons for supposing that belief to be true. The belief does not, however, follow from the reasons; the reasons follow from the belief. They are mere "rationalizations" of a belief really held on irrational grounds. A sufficiently ingenious mind can rationalize any belief, however absurd. Some people can produce rationalizations for the belief that the Anglo-Saxon race are the ten lost tribes of Israel, others for the belief that the world is flat, others for the belief that the prosperity and the happiness of the people are secured by the unrestricted interplay of private interests in production and exchange. There is no belief so absurd that no one has found a rationalization for it.

We can all of us best deal with our prejudices by recognizing frankly that they are likely to play a large part in influencing our own opinions and by using such methods as we can to counteract their influence. They lead us, for example, to overlook fallacious thinking in writings or speeches we agree with, while they enable us readily to detect errors in what we disagree with. So, in all matters in which our emotions are strongly involved (either for or against), we must distrust our own judgments and compare them carefully with those of people who disagree with us. Our prejudices tend also to make us forget facts unfavorable to our opinions. Darwin records that he kept a notebook in which he jotted all facts or ideas which were opposed to his conclusions, because otherwise he forgot them. So it resulted that when he published his results, his opponents could bring forward few objections which he had not already considered himself.

One must be particularly cautious in quoting from memory any evidence in favor of a view one holds. I have frequently typed from an apparently vivid memory incidents recorded in books I had read, but on examining the books again before sending what I had written to be printed, I have found the original passages were very little like what I had quoted, and generally much less directly favorable to the view I was trying to support.

Serious errors of fact have crept into books in this way by authors writing in perfectly good faith. In the middle of the nineteenth century, highway robbers in Great Britain developed the unpleasant custom of garroting their victims until they were unconscious, a treatment which might lead to permanent injury or death. Parliament passed an Act in 1863 to punish garroting by flogging, but earlier in 1863, before this Act became effective, garroting had already been repressed by the severe application of the existing laws. Those who believe in flogging for criminal offenses often quote the suppression of garroting as an example of its successful use, although garroting was in fact put down without it. In the eleventh edition of the *Encyclopædia Britannica,* the author of the article on "Corporal Punishment" holds this view, and states that the Act for flogging garroters was passed in 1861—a mistake of two years which would strongly support his conclusion. Yet there is no possibility here of a deliberate falsification of dates. It was a mistake made in perfectly good faith.

There is another common fault in argument arising from the influence of prejudice which may be employed deliberately as a dishonest trick, but which more usually is the result of the speaker being himself blinded by his prejudices. This is the use in one context of an argument which would not be admitted in another context where it would lead to the opposite conclusion. This is "special pleading."

A clergyman, for example, who was actively engaged in trying to increase the stipends of poorly paid ministers, rebuked the coal miners for wanting an increase of wages because "five dollars a week more wages do not mean five dollars a week more happiness." Receivers of large unearned incomes are heard to deplore the sapping of rugged individualism by relief expenditures and public works. The construction of battleships is sometimes defended simply on the ground that it makes work—an argument which could

[157]

equally well be used in defense of building roads in excess of our requirements, making men shovel the sand from one point of our shore to another, or even (as Bernard Shaw has pointed out) as an encouragement to motorists to knock down pedestrians. It is quite reasonable to maintain that an increase of miners' wages and the payment of social security benefits are undesirable and that the building of battleships is a national necessity, but these are conclusions which cannot be supported by the arguments used unless one is willing to apply the same arguments to the other cases mentioned.

No one who has examined the repertory of arguments of the average man can fail to notice how persistently some are applied in one context and some in another. It is a good thing that he, himself, should have a large income because (a) the amount he saves increases the capital of the country, (b) the part he spends, even on luxuries, is good for trade and increases employment. It is good that his gardener's wages should be low because (c) the country cannot afford the burden of high wages, (d) poverty and hardship produce rugged, virile characters, and (e) if the gardener were paid more, he would only spend it on useless luxuries like going to the pictures. This is only a small sample of what one can draw from him in a few minutes' conversation, but it is enough to show the prevalence of special pleading. (b) and (e) are inconsistent with one another; the view that luxury expenditure is socially valuable being applied to himself, while the view that it is a social evil is applied to his gardener. (*a*) is not applied to his gardener, while (*c*) and (*d*) are not applied to himself. We may further ask whether he really believes (*a*) and (*e*), which imply that the thing of greatest social value to do with money is to save it, or (*b*) which implies that the right thing is to spend it on no matter what. It is useless to ask which he believes. He believes both propositions and will employ either in different contexts. Men have a much larger power of believing inconsistent propositions than is commonly supposed.

The obvious way to deal with special pleading is to get the person who is using this device to admit the general principle that underlies his particular argument and then to apply it to the particular cases he has ignored. A recent public speaker, for example, objected to proposed legislation for providing milk for poor children on the ground that it would make us a nation of milksops. One would need to ask the speaker whether all children who had a sufficiency of milk became milksops, which, if admitted, would lead to the further question, whether he would therefore deprive his own children of milk to insure that they did not become milksops. It would even be fair to ask whether the speaker had sufficient milk in his own childhood.

In trying to detect and undermine special pleading, one must be careful not to do one's opponent the injustice of attributing to him an extension (pp. 33–5) of his proposition. In the above case, for example, the speaker may not have intended to imply that all

[159]

children tend to become milksops by drinking sufficient milk, but only the children of the poor, or only if the milk were provided by the community. We must allow him to tell us what the general proposition is that he is prepared to defend, and then attack it either by making other particular applications which he will reject, or by showing its untruth in some other way.

Knowledge of the prejudices of his audience can, of course, be used by an orator in exactly the same way as knowledge of their habits of thought (Chapter Six). He can make easier the acceptance of a doubtful proposition by wording it in such a way as to make it appeal to the prejudices of his audience, or by introducing it only after the statement of a number of other propositions enthusiastically favored by their prejudices. These devices and the methods of dealing with them are essentially the same as have already been described in the chapter on thought habits, so they need not be dealt with here.

There is, however, a particular form of the first of these two devices which deserves fuller mention. That is the trick of commending or condemning a course of action because of its good or bad practical effects on the lives of one's hearers. A very considerable part of political propaganda is made up of this kind of appeal. Whether he is attacking national expenditure on armaments or on relief, a speaker can get a ready response by pointing to its effects in increased taxation. Our objection to increased taxation is primarily a very individual and personal one, that as we pay more in

[160]

taxes we have less to spend on ourselves and our families. Even when the speaker makes a relatively impersonal basis to his appeal by emphasizing the effect of high taxes as a burden on industry, we can safely guess that it is the effect on themselves that his audience are thinking about. That is the true reason for the success of the speaker in carrying conviction.

Yet each of the audience could, if he were sufficiently detached emotionally from his own affairs, truthfully reflect that its effect on himself is not the wise ground for deciding on national policy. It is unimportant from the point of view of the community as a whole whether the fifty dollars in his pocket is spent by himself or by the nation. Its expenditure by the nation will create as much employment as its expenditure by himself, and the important question is, which of the two ways of spending it will best promote the general good. In fact, he will not reason like this; an appeal to an audience to welcome with patriotic fervor a lowering of their own standard of living that will benefit the nation as a whole is an appeal that falls very flat. It is a peculiarity of the modern sentiment of patriotism that men can be persuaded to sacrifice their lives for their country but not the contents of their pockets.

When people first realize how many of their opinions and even of the reasoning processes by which they support them are based on known or unknown emotional foundations, they are sometimes led to conclude that they must therefore believe nothing at all. That, of course, is absurd. There must be right opinions even on questions in which the strength of our own emotional inclinations makes it most difficult to find these right opinions. There must be a best way of distributing wealth although it is ten to one that the fact that we are possessors or that we are not possessors of wealth ourselves will be the strongest influence in determining our opinion of what that best way is. Similarly, there must be an objectively true answer to the question as to whether at death we just disappear like candles blown out or whether we continue our conscious existence for all eternity. Yet which of us (whether believers or disbelievers in personal immortality) will suppose that he holds his opinions on the matter on grounds that are scientific and objective, and independent of his own feelings and desires?

The attitude of detachment of mind is one which can be cultivated and must be cultivated if we are to arrive at true conclusions on matters which touch us personally. The first step is to recognize the existence of this kind of irrational motivation in our own minds; then we can make allowances for it. If we are rich, we must try to force ourselves to think out social problems on general grounds without allowing ourselves to be influenced by our own powerful desire for the continuance of our own individual comfort and security. Whatever may be our individual circumstances, we must learn to adopt the same attitude toward the sorrows and pleasures of others as we do toward our own, and to adopt the same attitude toward our own sorrows and pleasures as we do toward

[162]

those of other people. Of course, that is hard, much harder to do than to say. So we must always be prepared to admit that our conclusions as to what is best for others may have really been dictated to us by consideration of what is best for ourselves. But we can and must do our best to detach ourselves from our own irrational motivations of opinion. The first step in that detachment is to recognize them.

Nor must we make the foolish mistake of supposing that we can settle controversies by attributing prejudices to our opponents and by labeling their arguments "rationalizations." Some people seem to think that it is a sufficient argument against socialism to say that it is based on the envy of those without possessions for those with, and that its intellectual defense is just a rationalization of this envy. This is no more reasonable than the opposite argument that conservatism is merely based on the determination of the possessors to stick to what they have got, and that its intellectual defense is simply a rationalization of this determination. Undoubtedly the desire of the poor for wealth and of the wealthy for a continuance of their wealth are powerful motive forces behind the belief in socialism and in capitalism respectively. But having made all allowances for the strength of whichever of these prejudices our own circumstances have given us, the question remains—which is the better system? That is a question we cannot settle by discussing the prejudices of our opponents. A true opinion as well as a false one may owe much of its strength to irrational motives.

CHAPTER TWELVE

The Need For Straight Thinking

So far, we have spent most of our time considering "crooked thinking." Now let us turn to the other side of the question and consider what is straight thinking. The supreme example of straight thinking is provided by science. The scientist weighs, measures, and calculates without any use of emotional phraseology, guided only by a simple creed of the universality of the law of cause and effect.

The scientist's method is justified, for its application gives us ever more and more knowledge. Results obtained one day point to a conception which it may be possible to express in simple terms, or, on the other hand, may be expressible in abstruse mathematical formulae understood by only a few people. In either case, acceptance of this conception leads to new experiments giving new knowledge not guessed at the time of the original experiment. New results cause old conceptions to be modified, so all conceptions are held tentatively. Yet the progress of scientific thought is never backward. The new conception still expresses the old truth, but it expresses also something more. Science gives us an ever-widening circle of knowledge.

[164]

⎣Where scientific methods have been applied to practical problems, they give us ever-increasing control of our environment⎦ Before the application of scientific methods to a particular practical problem we are at the mercy of blind forces. Where we begin to apply scientific methods, these forces begin to come under our control. The ideal of straight thinking must be the application of the scientific habit of thought to all our practical problems, and the replacement of blind forces controlling our destinies by our own intelligent and conscious control. In some fields we have already begun to apply this conscious control. Many of the diseases which at one time were blind forces under which we bowed (as we now submit ourselves to earthquakes, thunderstorms, and trade depressions) have now begun to be brought under conscious control by the development of the science of medicine.

Until the last war we believed in leaving the rivalry between the interests of various nations as blind and uncontrolled forces. Only a few cranks believed that men should attempt to bring them under conscious control. When these forces led to the soaking of the world in blood by a disaster which injured the victorious nations no less than the conquered, we made the League of Nations and in the Kellogg treaties a beginning (a very small beginning) at the attempt to control them. Yet modern nations are far from prepared to give up their sovereignty to a superstate whose aim would be the scientific understanding of the processes of international rivalry and the exercise of an authority over all nations which would rob these processes of their power to produce war.

Still less do we believe in the scientific understanding and control of the economic processes in a single country by which its goods are given in extravagant abundance to a few, while, in the words of President Roosevelt, "one third of the nation is ill-housed, ill-fed, ill-clad." These processes remain the product of the blind interaction of the individual interests of different merchants and buyers, of employers of labor and manual workers. There is little attempt at conscious control. Political economy remains largely a theoretical science.

Let us compare our attitude toward such questions with our attitude toward disease. The man who brings a scientific attitude of mind to the analysis of a dispute between his own country and another is labeled a "traitor." In politics we are told that we should distrust "logic" (by which is meant the coldly scientific approach to problems which is the only certain way of solving them), and trust to our instincts or to horse trading. When we suggest that poverty is an evil whose causes must be discovered and, at all costs, removed, we are told that the life of societies follows unchangeable economic laws with which it is dangerous to tamper.

It is true that social life follows economic laws just as an automobile obeys mechanical laws and the human body obeys physiological laws. But we are not content to say that an automobile must follow mechanical laws and then leave it to go where it likes. On the contrary, we move its steering wheel and its throttle until we have produced conditions under which the iron mechanical laws it obeys carry it where we want at the speed we want. We do not consider it dangerous to interfere with the conditions in which its mechanical laws work. We get rid of that danger by understanding these laws. As to the danger of interfering with the conditions under which economic laws act, we may well ask whether it is not much more dangerous to leave them uncontrolled when we see the terrible effects in human misery which follow at present from their action.

Why should we adopt toward these problems an attitude so different from our attitude toward illness? In the course of ages, scientific methods have slowly replaced other methods in the treatment of disease, and, as a result, a very large part of disease has come under our control, and this part is always increasing. When we are ill and call in a doctor, he does not encourage us to hope that we shall muddle through. He seeks for the cause of our condition—whether it is a germ infection, an internal injury, or just a set of ideas in our own mind—and he tries to remove that cause. He does not doubt that in sickness as in health our bodies obey physiological laws. He is not, however, content simply to say that and do nothing about it. By medicine, by surgical operation, or by other treatment, he puts our bodies in conditions in which physiological laws will work for and not against our health.

Behind his work is that of a great army of research

workers who have made his treatment of us possible. These have not attacked the abuses of microbes in emotionally colored phrases; they have instead impartially studied their habits and conditions of life. They have shown no reverence for modes of treatment (like bleeding) which merely have the recommendation that they are old. They have boldly challenged every ancient habit of thought in the science of healing until it has proved itself to be of value.

Our own individual illnesses can be cured by scientific methods. The diseases of the great society to which we belong cannot be so healed because we distrust the cool impartial voice of science in national and international affairs.

It is as if we were all travelers in an automobile traveling at speed over an unmapped plain. The driver has not his hands on the wheel, for he knows neither where he wants to go nor how to get there if he did. When we suggest he should put his hands on the wheel and exercise his intelligence in thinking where he wants to go and how to get there, he turns to us with an idiotic smile and says that the car must obey mechanical laws and that we must trust our instinct for muddling through. We know that the plain through which we are traveling has ravines and morasses in which lie the wrecked remains of cars which have traveled blindly across it in times long past. Occasionally we come into collision with other automobiles, but such collisions fill the survivors with such exalted emotions and are believed to be productive of such extraordinary virtues that no one

blames the driver for the deaths of some of the passengers and the grave injuries to the automobile.

Occasionally the passengers are allowed to decide
who shall have the privilege of sitting in front of the
steering wheel, but as they too do not believe in intelligent choice of route and know even less than the
driver how to get there, and since the new driver may
also sit with his hands off the wheel, these occasional
lapses into apparently democratic control have little
practical importance. Yet one does hear voices protesting that an automobile can be driven in safety
only by conscious and intelligent control, that their
experience of automobile driving has shown them that
there is no such thing as an instinct for muddling
through, that the relaxation of intelligent control
means inevitable disaster, and that an automobile
which is allowed to obey merely mechanical laws
obeys them by crashing.

What will happen to that automobile in which we
are all traveling I do not know. Perhaps the mechanic
will push the driver to one side and himself place his
hands on the wheel. He too may bring us to disaster
through not knowing how to drive, but the disaster
will be somewhat less certain than if we hope to muddle through. Our better chance of success is if we all
apply to national and international affairs conscious
control and intelligent thought. We can solve the
problems of war and poverty if we approach them in
the same scientific spirit as we have now learned to
apply to disease, sure that every effect has a cause,
and that impartial scientific investigation will reveal

[169]

those causes and that sufficiently determined effort will remove them.

A really educated democracy, distrustful of emotional phraseology and all the rest of the stock in trade of the exploiters of crooked thinking, devoid of reverence for ancient institutions and ancient ways of thinking, could take conscious control of our social development and could destroy these plagues of our civilizations—war, poverty, and crime—if it were determined that nothing should stand in the way of their removal—no old traditions and none of the ancient privileges which are called "rights" by their holders. That would be a beneficent revolution which we can have if we are willing to trust our own intelligences sufficiently boldly and if we want it badly enough. But the revolution must start in our own minds.

Thirty-Four Dishonest Tricks Which Are Commonly Used in Argument, With the Methods of Overcoming Them

IN most textbooks of logic there is to be found a list of "fallacies," classified in accordance with the logical principles they violate. Such collections are interesting and important, and it is to be hoped that any readers who wish to go more profoundly into the principles of logical thought will turn to these works. The present list is, however, something quite different. Its aim is practical and not theoretical. It is intended to be a list which can be conveniently used for detecting dishonest modes of thought which we shall actually meet in arguments and speeches. Sometimes more than one of the tricks mentioned would be classified by the logician under one heading, some he would omit altogether, while others that he would put in are not be found here. Practical convenience and practical importance are the criteria I have used in this list.

If we have a plague of flies in the house we buy fly-papers and not a treatise on the zoological classification of *Musca domestica* and related species. This implies no sort of disrespect for zoologists, or for the value of their work as a first step in the effective control of flies. The present book bears to the treatises of logicians the relationship of flypaper to zoological classifications.

(1) *The use of emotionally toned words* (pp. 3–19).

Dealt with by translating the statement into words emotionally neutral.

(2) *Making a statement in which "all" is implied but "some" is true* (pp. 20–30).

Dealt with by putting the word "all" into the statement and showing that it is then false.

(3) *Proof by selected instances* (p. 31).

Dealt with dishonestly by selecting instances opposing your opponent's contention or honestly by pointing out the true form of the proof (as a statistical problem in association) and either supplying the required numerical facts or pointing out that your opponent has not got them.

(4) *Extension of an opponent's proposition by contradiction or by misrepresentation of it* (pp. 33–5).

Dealt with by stating again the more moderate position which is being defended.

[172]

(5) *Evasion of a sound refutation of an argument by the use of a sophistical formula* (pp. 35 and 36).

Dealt with by analysis of the formula and demonstration of its unsoundness.

(6) *Diversion to another question, to a side issue, or by irrelevant objection* (pp. 36–40).

Dealt with by refusing to be diverted from the original question, but stating again the real question at issue.

(7) *Proof by inconsequent argument* (pp. 40–42).

Dealt with by asking that the connection between the proposition and the alleged proof may be explained, even though the request for explanation may be attributed to ignorance or lack of logical insight on the part of the person making it.

(8) *The recommendation of a position because it is a mean between two extremes* (pp. 42–6).

Dealt with by denying the usefulness of the principle as a method of discovering the truth. In practice, this can most easily be done by showing that our own view also can be represented as a mean between two extremes.

(9) *The use of a syllogism with undistributed middle term or other argument of unsound form* (pp. 47–53).

Since the unsoundness of such arguments can be easily seen when the form of the argument is clearly

[173]

displayed, an opponent who does this can be dealt with by making such a simple statement of his argument that its unsoundness is apparent. For one's own satisfaction when reading an argument of doubtful soundness, the same object can sometimes be attained by making a diagram.

(10) *Argument in a circle* (p. 53–4).

(11) *Begging the question* (pp. 53, 54–6).
Both 10 and 11 must be dealt with in the same way as 9; by restating your opponent's argument in such a simple way that the nature of the device used must be clear to anyone.

(12) *Suggestion by repeated affirmation* (pp. 58–60).

(13) *Suggestion by use of a confident manner* (p. 60).

(14) *Suggestion by prestige* (pp. 61–3, 67).
The best safeguard against all three of these tricks of suggestion is a theoretical knowledge of suggestion, so that their use may be detected. All three devices lose much of their effect if the audience sees how the effect is being obtained. Ridicule is often used too to undermine the confident manner, or any kind of criticism which makes the speaker begin to grow angry or plaintive.

[174]

(15) *Prestige by false credentials* (p. 63).

The obvious remedy for this is, when practicable, to expose the falsity of the titles, degrees, etc., that are used. The prestige then collapses.

(16) *Prestige by the use of pseudotechnical jargon* (pp. 63–7).

Best dealt with by asking in a modest manner that the speaker should explain himself more simply.

(17) *Affectation of failure to understand backed by prestige* (pp. 67–8).

Dealt with by more than ample explanation.

(18) *The use of questions drawing out damaging admissions* (pp. 68–9).

Dealt with by refusal to make the admissions. The difficulty of this refusal must be overcome by any device reducing one's suggestibility to the questioner.

(19) *The appeal to mere authority* (pp. 72–3).

Dealt with by considering whether the person supposed to have authority had a sound reason for making the assertion which is attributed to him.

(20) *Overcoming resistance to a doubtful proposition by a preliminary statement of a few easily accepted ones* (pp. 77–8, 160).

Knowledge of this trick and preparedness for it are the best safeguard against its effects.

(21) *Statement of a doubtful proposition in such a way that it fits in with the thought habits or the prejudices of the hearer* (pp. 77–9, 160).

A habit of questioning what appears obvious is the best safeguard against this trick. A particular device of value against it is to restate a questionable proposition in a new context in which one's thought habits do not lead to its acceptance.

(22) *The use of generally accepted tabloids of thought as premises in argument* (pp. 92–9).

There is no satisfactory way of dealing with tabloid thinking in argument except to point out good-humoredly and with a backing of real evidence that matters are more complicated than your opponent supposes.

(23) *"There is much to be said on both sides; so I shall make no decision either way," or any other formula leading to academic detachment from practical life* (pp. 100–101).

Dealt with by pointing out that taking no action has practical consequences no less real than those which result from acting on either of the propositions in dispute, and that this is no more likely than any other to be the right solution of the difficulty.

(24) *Argument by imperfect analogy* (pp. 110–14).

Dealt with by examining the alleged analogy in detail and pointing out where it breaks down.

[176]

(25) *Argument by forced analogy* (pp. 114–18).
The absurdity of a forced analogy can best be exposed by showing how many other analogies supporting different conclusions might have been used.

(26) *The use of a dilemma which ignores a continuous series of possibilities between the two extremes presented* (pp. 119–27).
Dealt with by refusing to accept either alternative, but pointing to the fact of the continuity which the person using the argument has ignored. Since this is likely to appear oversubtle to an opponent using the argument, it may be strengthened by pointing out that the argument is the same as that of saying, "Is this paper black or white?" when it is, in fact, a shade of gray.

(27) *The use of the fact of continuity between them to throw doubt on a real difference between two things (the "argument of the beard")* (pp. 127–9).
Dealt with by pointing out that the difference is nevertheless real. This again may be made stronger by pointing out that application of the same method of argument would deny the difference between "black" and "white" or between "hot" and "cold."

(28) *Illegitimate use of or demand for definition* (pp. 129–31).
If an opponent uses definitions to produce clear-cut conceptions for facts which are not clear cut, it is necessary to point out to him how much more com-

[177]

plicated facts are in reality than in his thought. If he tries to drive you to define for the same purpose, the remedy is to refuse formal definition but to adopt some other method of making your meaning clear.

(29) *Ambiguity, vagueness, or meaninglessness in the terms used in argument* (pp. 132–9).

Dealt with by continually demanding explanation until the terms become clear, or by proffering such explanation yourself and asking your opponent if that is what he means, then going over the argument again with the terms clarified. With a persistently confused thinker this remedy may be useless; nothing will drive him to think clearly. The only remedy is not to argue with him.

(30) *Speculative argument* (pp. 140–46).

Rebutted by pointing out that what is cannot be inferred from what ought to be or from what the speaker feels must be.

(31) *Angering an opponent in order that he may argue badly* (pp. 151–2).

Dealt with by refusing to get angry however annoying our opponent may be.

(32) *Special pleading* (pp. 157–60).

Dealt with by applying one's opponent's special arguments to other propositions which he is unwilling to admit.

[178]

(33) *Commending or condemning a proposition because of its practical consequences to the hearer* (pp. 160–63).

We can only become immune from the effect of this kind of appeal if we have formed a habit of recognizing our own tendencies to be guided by our prejudices and by our own self-interest, and of distrusting our judgment on questions in which we are practically concerned.

(34) *Argument by attributing prejudices or motives to one's opponent* (p. 163).

Best dealt with by pointing out that other prejudices may equally well determine the opposite view, and that, in any case, the question of why a person holds an opinion is an entirely separate one from the question of whether that opinion is a right one (which is the question at issue).

A Discussion Illustrating Crooked Thinking

IN order to illustrate the foregoing list of dishonest arguments I have devised an imaginary conversation between three gentlemen in which as many dishonest devices as possible are used. The three disputants are supposed to be of reasonably good intelligence and intellectual honesty and to be using the devices without any conscious intention of scoring an unfair victory. The arguments have been chosen to illustrate crooked thinking, so that the whole conversation is worse than an average sample of intellectual after-dinner discussion. Most of the arguments, however, are identical with or similar in form to ones that I have heard used by quite intelligent people. I do not think that any part of the conversation is more crooked and unsound than can be heard at any place where intellectual conversation is carried on, although I admit that it would be difficult to find, in practice, a conversation in which there is so sustained a failure to argue straight on any problem. To that extent the conversation is a caricature, but a caricature made up of natural fragments.

I suggest that, at a first reading, readers should cover up my notes on the conversation, and write down all the pieces of crooked argumentation or thought that they can detect in the passage, referring when possible to numbers in the list of dishonest tricks in Appendix One. Afterward they may wish to compare the fallacies they have detected with those pointed out in my notes. My notes do not claim to be either exhaustive or unprejudiced, and many readers will no doubt make a different list which has the same claim to be considered right as my own.

Those taking part in the conversation are B——— a businessman, P——— a professor, and C——— a clergyman. They are sitting together after a dinner at B———'s home. The conversation is opened by the professor.

P. I wonder what the result of the election will be.

B. A return to a sound and sensible business government, I trust. What the country needs now is a period of tranquillity, so that it can get back to prosperity.[1]

Another glass of grape juice, Professor. C———, you know, is one of these radicals, but I assume you will vote Republican.

P. As a scientist, I find myself in disagreement with

---

[1] B——— makes free use of emotionally toned words (No. 1). "Sound" and "sensible" have more of emotional meaning than of any other. A government which appears "sound and sensible" to its supporters will be called "conventional and uninspired" by its opponents. Similarly "tranquillity" has the same objective meaning as "stagnation," but an opposite emotional meaning.

all political parties. All seem to me to be equally un-scientific. The vital problems of finding outlets for our expanding population and of weeding out the unfit can only be solved by the application of the scientific method to political problems. At present, I see no signs of any of the political parties realizing this vital necessity, so I shall refrain from using my vote.[2]

C. No, no more for me, thank you.

As a minister of the Gospel,[3] it seems to me that the great problem before us is the uplifting of the laboring masses.[4] I put my trust in an enlightened and Christianized socialism.[5] I realize very well that the Socialist Party is not ideal, but purified from its materialism . . .

B. [interrupting]. But what you don't realize, my dear fellow, is that its aims are materialist through

[2] This is an example of an intellectual justification of academic detachment from practical life (No. 23). P—— is probably a man of higher intellectual ability than either of the others, but the practical outcome of his intellectual powers, so far as they affect the election, is the same as would result from his being too imbecile to find his way to the polling booth. His academic detachment is also shown by the two "vital problems" he mentions; they do not include the problem of securing that people have enough to eat.

Notice too that he begins by appealing to his prestige as a scientist (No. 14).

[3] He too begins by appealing to his prestige (No. 14).

[4] Here we first see one of the most striking features of the whole speech—its extreme vagueness (No. 29). "Uplifting" is a word used without any very precise meaning; so also is "materialism."

[5] Begging the question by the use of the emotionally toned word "enlightened" (No. 11), B—— would not regard any socialism as enlightened.

and through.[6] Fill the worker's belly [7] and never mind his soul. That's not Christianity. There would be no room for parsons in the socialist state.[8]

P. I have no objection to filling a man's belly. Our own are full, and we are the better for it.[9] I should fill every worker's belly, but I have no patience with this socialistic [10] proposal to give a handout to bums: [11] a sentimental [12] policy that some members of your party would land us in, B——.

[6] The word "materialist" as used by C—— has, as we have seen, no exact meaning. But C—— has made it clear that he has thought habits in connection with it, so B—— takes advantage of those thought habits to advance his own view (No. 21).

[7] B—— might well be charged with special pleading (No. 32) in this part of the second sentence. He has just been very much occupied with the business of filling his own belly without feeling that it was a reprehensible aim.

"Filling the belly" is a phrase with strong emotional meaning of disapprobation (No. 1). The emotionally neutral phrase would be "give the worker enough to eat."

[8] Appealing to the practical interests of C—— (No. 33).

[9] P—— deals with B——'s special pleading in the way recommended in Appendix One—by applying the same words to other circumstances in which B—— would not maintain his attitude of disapproval. He does not destroy the effect of B——'s emotional term "filling the belly" by translating it into an emotionally neutral phrase, but robs it of its emotional implications just as effectively by applying it to their own dining.

[10] The termination "-ic" gives this word an emotional tone of disapproval (No. 1). C—— would have said "socialist." With the same effect one can say "capitalistic," "atheistic," "militaristic," etc.

[11] A tabloid much oversimplifying a complicated social policy (No. 22). Using also two words with strong emotional tone (No. 1).

[12] Another emotionally toned word (No. 1). Equivalent words with the opposite emotional tone are "kindly" or "humane." To make the statement emotionally neutral, the word should be omitted altogether.

[183]

B. Of course we may have to pay unemployment insurance to workers who have been thrown out of employment by no fault of their own.[13] No government could let the unemployed starve. But we cannot increase taxation which is already as much as the industries of the country could stand. Rob [14] the industrious and give the money to bums, that's the socialist policy all the time. The workers themselves will be the first to suffer when the country is ruined. Look at Russia, where the workers have been underfed ever since the Bolsheviks took control.

P. I am very skeptical of these stories of starvation in Russia. We have heard them ever since the revolution. There seem to be plenty of Russian workers still alive who can hardly have been starving for the last fourteen years.[15] Starvation is generally a pretty quick death. What is the evidence for starvation in Russia at the present time?

B. Well, there's a pretty strict censorship in Russia but stories keep coming through. I can't quote you any definite cases, but there must be some foundation for these stories. Where there's smoke, there's fire [16]

[13] Dealing with P——'s use of the emotional phrase "handout to bums" by the method of translating it into emotionally neutral language.

[14] Another emotional word (No. 1). "Tax" would be the neutral equivalent.

[15] A flagrant extension of his opponent's proposition (No. 4). B—— said only that the workers had been underfed; P—— is arguing against the proposition that they were starving (*i.e.* that they had insufficient food to maintain life).

[16] Instead of avoiding P——'s extension by restating his original position, B—— tacitly accepts it and brings forward a

[with increasing irritation].[17] Anyhow, there's the definite case of the great famine in 1932, brought about by the ruthlessness of the Bolsheviks in their dealings with the peasants.[18] Do you deny that, Professor? I can't understand a man of high ideals like yourself defending these blackguards.[19] You don't deny, I suppose, that they murdered the Czar and everyone they could lay hands on who disagreed with their politics.[20]

P. I am not defending the Bolsheviks and I don't

very weak line of argument in its defense. This is the device of using a sophistical formula (No. 5) to justify the holding of an opinion as certain on admittedly bad evidence. No amount of bad evidence can give a reasonably certain conclusion as suggested by the formula, "where there's smoke, there's fire."

[17] Rising anger indicates that B—— is becoming conscious of the weakness of the position he is defending. It is weak, but only because he has unwittingly accepted P——'s extension, instead of sticking to his first statement.

[18] Here he tries to force an extension on P—— (No. 4). What P—— maintained was that the Russian workers had not been starving all the time since the revolution—a statement so obvious as to be hardly worth making, particularly since it was not a contradiction of B——'s statement that they had been underfed. Here, however, B—— is arguing as if P—— had made the more extreme statement that they had never been starving since the revolution.

[19] The accusation of "defending the Bolsheviks" shows a background of tabloid thinking (Chapter Seven). P——, in fact, denies one particular statement about the Bolsheviks (as we have seen, a statement which no one else has made), but B—— feels that the statements against the Bolsheviks must be considered as a single block. All must be accepted or the speaker is guilty of "defending the Bolsheviks."

[20] Clearly a diversion (No. 6). Whatever may be the truth or importance of the facts stated, they are not inconsistent with P——'s statement.

[185]

deny the reality of the great famine of 1932.[21] I merely said that the Russian workers have not been starving all the time since the revolution. However, I hold no brief for Bolshevism, which seems to me to be a detestable [22] system. I am content with our individualist industrial system.

C. [slowly and impressively]. No man should be content with our industrialism while one child living under that system is short of food.[23]

B. My dear C——, certainly no one wants children to starve. Industrialism does more toward feeding children than all the socialistic theories in the world.[24]

[21] Correctly refusing to accept either B——'s extension or his diversion.

[22] A perfectly legitimate use of an emotionally colored word. P—— is reporting his own personal reaction to Bolshevism and is not claiming to give an objective account of it.

[23] Whatever we may think of the matter of this remark, we must notice that the manner of its delivery is that of suggestion by the use of a confident manner (No. 13).

Also we may ask why children are brought into the argument. Middle-aged people are also short of food. It may truly be argued that undernutrition has worse effects on children than on those in later life, but that is not why C—— mentioned children. He is taking advantage of emotional habits of thought in connection with children (No. 21). In the same way a believer in nonresistance to evil is asked: "Wouldn't you consider it right to use force to protect a helpless little child who was being maltreated by a powerful and brutal man?" He is never asked the equally reasonable question: "Wouldn't you consider it right to use force to protect a helpless middle-aged stockbroker who was being maltreated by a powerful and brutal man?"

[24] This argument depends on an ambiguity in the use of the word "industrialism" (No. 29). B—— appears to be using it as equivalent to "industry," while C—— used it for the particular

How many children could the Socialist Party feed? [25]

C. I hold no brief for any particular political party,[26] but I expect the Socialist Party would do as much or as little in direct relief of poverty as any other political party.[27]

P. Let us return to a point in the argument which interests me more than the merits or demerits of the Socialist Party. You both seem to agree that children ought not to be starving. As a scientist,[28] I cannot agree with you. Nature effects all improvements in the race by a process of elimination of the unfit by natural selection. By natural selection, the horse has become strong and the greyhound swift. Starvation is one of Nature's weapons for eliminating the unfit.[29]

conditions under which industry takes place at the present time. The feeding of children would certainly not go on without "industry" in the general sense, but it is not, therefore, dependent on any particular conditions under which industry takes place.

[25] Another diversion (No. 6). This is also an example of special pleading (No. 32), for no political party feeds children.

[26] Instead of challenging B——'s statement that industrialism feeds children, C—— follows the diversion, and takes refuge in a characteristic vagueness. When defending socialism, he does not mean any particular socialist organization. If he were pressed by B——, it would probably become clear that he is similarly not prepared to defend any particular socialist proposal.

[27] Not content with the evasion by vagueness, he successfully meets his opponent's special pleading in the usual manner.

[28] Again he appeals to prestige authority (No. 14). Much of what he is about to say would hardly pass muster without some such support.

[29] The preceding three sentences are ordinarily accepted commonplaces of evolutionary biology. Their function in the argu-

The sight of her methods may offend our humaner feelings, but the attempt of sentimental philanthropy to interfere with them can only lead to degeneration of the human race.[30] Soup kitchens and the provision of free milk for children are biological crimes.

C. [after a pause]. Is the swiftness of the greyhound the result of natural selection? [31] You surprise me, Professor; I thought that it was a result of breeding.[32]

P. Say the wolf, then. The argument remains the same.[33] I want to see a race that has the biological virtues of strength, fitness, and independence.

---

ment is that of the few easily accepted propositions which overcome the resistance to a highly questionable one which follows (No. 20). They are not, as may be supposed at first sight, logical steps leading up to the conclusions, for the conclusion to which they should lead is not that the intensive starvation of poor children should go on unchecked (which is the proposition that P—— is defending), but that all children should be starved sufficiently to cause the death of the physically unfit. The statement about the horse and the greyhound is also an imperfect analogy (No. 24).

[30] Again P—— uses very improperly the emotionally toned word "sentimental" (No. 1). If a given kind of philanthropy leads to degeneration of the human race, then that kind of philanthropy can fairly be called "sentimental," but not otherwise. The word should not be used in the course of an argument intended to prove that such philanthropy leads to racial degeneration.

[31] C—— attempts a diversion by irrelevant objection (No. 6).

[32] The sarcastic form of this remark is calculated to anger P—— (No. 31).

[33] P—— refuses to accept C——'s diversion or to become angry. It was, of course, his blunder that made the irrelevant objection possible.

[188]

C. I suppose the tapeworm and the liver fluke become parasitic by natural selection? [34]

P. Yes, if you like.[35] Man is not a tapeworm or liver fluke.[36]

C. By what right do you call the children of the unemployed "the unfit"? [37] As a minister of the Gospel,[38] I protest against any such statement. In the homes of the poor in my parish I find a level of spiritual attainment far higher than is to be found among the rich.[39]

[34] Showing the imperfection of P——'s analogy of the effect of natural selection on the horse, etc., by the expedient of suggesting that the same analogy with different terms would point to an opposite conclusion.

[35] A form of words unfairly suggesting the unimportance of C——'s objection.

[36] Meaning, of course, that man does not resemble these creatures sufficiently for the purpose of analogy—a dishonest evasion of C——'s point that the results of natural selection are not always desirable. P—— is saying in effect: "Your analogy is imperfect," as if C—— were bringing forward a new argument by analogy of his own, whereas he is really pointing to an imperfection in P——'s previous argument by analogy. This is an example of an inconsequent argument (No. 7), since it does not really meet C——'s point, but only appears to do so.

[37] Here C—— puts his finger on the worst weakness of P——'s argument. That those on whom starvation presses hardly in conditions of unemployment are the unfit in the biological sense is an unproved assumption which only needs dragging into the limelight to be disposed of. It is essential to P——'s argument, for without it the abolition of the philanthropy he condemns would not lead to a process of natural selection.

[38] C—— has made a perfectly good point and has no need to support it with prestige suggestion (No. 14).

[39] Still less should he support it by an extreme statement which, if true, would be inconsequent (No. 7), but which is

P. I am not a minister of the Gospel but a mere scientist, and I must confess that I have no very clear idea as to what is meant by a "level of spiritual attainment." [40] So far as my inexpert observations go, I have not noticed the superiority you refer to.[41]

As to the relationship between poverty and unfitness, I regard poverty itself as a mark of biological unfitness. It is a failure of social adaptation. The socially maladapted are the biologically unfit. The unemployed are those who have been unable to adapt themselves to the condition of the society in which they live. They are biologically unfit because they are socially maladapted.[42]

C. My training has been in philosophy rather than science, and I fear I am unable to carry on a discus-

no more likely to be true than its opposite, and is open to the objection that "spiritual attainment" is something too vague to be made the subject of a quantitative statement. C—— has, in fact, made a diversion very unfavorable to himself.

[40] This is the trick of affectation of ignorance backed by prestige (No. 17). The word "mere" is ironical and must not blind us to the fact that P—— is again calling attention to his prestige as scientist. He is saying in effect: "I am a learned man but I cannot understand you; you must be talking nonsense."

[41] Not content with this, he also denies C——'s alleged fact. For the moment he accepts C——'s diversion, since it gives him the opportunity of scoring a cheap victory.

[42] The substitution of "social maladaptation" for "unfitness" makes his remarks sound more scientific, but it does not really get over the difficulty. He is relying on the prestige effect of technical jargon (No. 16).

Realizing the weakness of this substitution, he uses another trick—repeated affirmation (No. 12). He says it four times.

sion in the barbarous jargon of the modern scientist.[43] Perhaps you would be good enough to define for us this term "social maladaptation." [44]

B. But seriously, Professor.[45] Do you mean that biology would have us let the unemployed and their families starve?

P. I do not say that our superfluous population should be allowed to starve.[46] The remedy which biology suggests is that they should never be allowed to be born.

---

[43] In a slightly different form, this is essentially the same trick of affecting ignorance (No. 17) as was used by P——.

[44] If C—— means to press for a formally correct definition (as he probably does) this is an example of an unfair badgering to define (No. 28). P—— could fairly be asked to explain what he means, but is unlikely to be able to provide a formally correct definition on the spur of the moment. If he could, it would give the idea more precision and rigidity than the facts it is trying to describe, for in fact social maladaptation is a phenomenon showing continuous variation. We are all more or less imperfectly fitted to our social environments, and there is no sharp point at which this imperfection becomes so great as to amount to social maladaptation.

[45] Fortunately B—— intervenes and prevents the discussion from being diverted to a somewhat personal squabble about science and philosophy. His first words are a mere verbal habit with hardly any meaning. He does not suppose that P—— and C—— have been joking.

[46] Actually, this is precisely what he did say; he is now making a diversion (No. 6) to a much more defensible position. He is using the trick of first stating an extreme position and then making a diversion to a more moderate one. P—— covers the diversion by simply denying what he previously said. He is no longer defending the unchecked operation of natural selection but the attempt to achieve its ends by other less painful methods. A very considerable shifting of the ground of debate!

B. But here they are; they have been born.[47] What are we to do about it if we don't feed them? What's your solution?

P. Effective control of our birth rate from the lower strata of society is the only possible solution. Then there would be no surplus population to bother about.[48] At present we are breeding from the dregs of the nation. The degraded and criminal elements in our population are increasing at an enormous rate, while the birth rate of the intelligent and industrious is falling.[49] I see nothing but disaster in front of our race if this process is allowed to go on unchecked.

[47] B—— attempts to check the diversion and to go on discussing the same problem.

[48] P—— gives further evidence of his academic detachment from practical affairs. He refuses to consider the practical problem which is worrying B——, which, however, would still exist for twenty years or so even if P——'s solution were put into practice immediately and proved effective.

[49] P——'s rapid shifts from "the unemployed" to "the socially maladapted" to "the dregs of the nation," and finally to "the degraded and criminal elements in the population," with no indication that he realizes he is changing the subject of discussion, shows a background of tabloid thinking (Chapter Seven). All of these different groupings of men are fused under a general idea (such as that of the "lower classes") with all the very important differences left out.

Also we notice another minor diversion (No. 6). He started by talking about that part of the population which becomes unemployed, but goes on to discuss the different problem of the relatively lower birth rate of the middle classes (who are meant to be indicated by the term "intelligent and industrious"). This is clearly a different problem, for an increase of birth rate among the middle classes could not be expected to reduce unemployment, but would rather tend to increase it, whatever other good effects it might have.

C. And you propose to stop this by interference with the natural rate of reproduction?

P. How else?

C. It would be an outrage to human dignity to apply the methods of the stud farm to the sacred function of human parenthood.[50] I cannot discuss such a subject.[51] It is a proposal that is offensive to every enlightened conscience.[52]

P. Why?

C. Because it is opposed to natural morality. It is an interference with Nature.[53] Man would not have been given an instinct to reproduce his kind if he had been intended to interfere with the results of that instinct.[54]

P. Aren't tilling the ground and giving medicine to

[50] An argument which depends entirely on emotionally toned words (No. 1).

[51] This is obvious. If C—— could transcend the limitations of his thought habits (Chapter Six) sufficiently to consider P——'s proposition as a possibility, he would be able to attack it more effectively.

[52] Begging the question by the use of an emotionally toned word (No. 11). He means by an "enlightened" conscience, one to which the proposal was offensive. P——, on the other hand, would regard a conscience as enlightened if the proposal were acceptable to it.

[53] Special pleading (No. 32), because C—— would not accept the general proposition that any interference with Nature was wrong, and has given no further objection to this particular interference with Nature which would make it wrong while others were right.

[54] A speculative argument (No. 30). C—— is arguing not from what is but from what must be. Also another bad specimen of special pleading; C—— would certainly not believe that a man must never interfere with what results from his instincts.

the sick interferences with Nature? [55] You give free milk to the illegitimate child of criminal parents, and then, when he follows the only course of behavior possible to anyone with his heredity,[56] you interfere with Nature by electrocuting him. Wouldn't it have been better to have interfered with Nature earlier on and sterilized his father? Remember that if you had started with his chromosomes you would have been just as bad a criminal.

C. I cannot accept such an account of human nature. It undermines the foundations of morality.[57] Either every man is a free agent and accountable for all his actions to the God who made him, or else he is the helpless victim of his heredity and there is no goodness or heroism in the world.[58] As a Christian philosopher,[59] I accept the first of these alternatives.

---

[55] P—— deals with C——'s special pleading in the manner recommended in Appendix One.

[56] Here, and again in the last sentence, P—— puts forward an extreme statement where a moderate one is true (No. 2). He says in effect: "All persons with criminal heredity become criminals," whereas the only justifiable statement is that there is a tendency for persons with criminal heredity to become criminals.

[57] Condemning the proposition as untrue, not because the evidence is against it but because of its practical consequences (No. 33).

[58] Presenting two extreme alternatives, whereas in fact there are an infinite number of possibilities lying in between these two extremes (No. 26). Most sensible people would, I think, accept one of the intermediate positions.

[59] Again appealing to his prestige. In point of fact, C——'s grounds for regarding himself as a philosopher are very slender. He attended classes in philosophy at Harvard twenty years ago and has read a few of the more conventional books on philos-

P. Well, what would you do with the child with a criminal heredity? Are you in favor of rearing him at public expense and hanging him when he grows up? [60]

C. I should remove him from poverty and bring him up in a comfortable Christian home. Then I do not believe that a child with what you call a "criminal heredity" would be any more likely to become a criminal than any other child. It is poverty and bad conditions of environment that make criminals, not heredity.[61] Destroy poverty and you need not bother about criminal tendencies in chromosomes.[62]

ophy which have been published since. This may, therefore, fairly be classed as an appeal to prestige based on false credentials (No. 15).

[60] A question designed to draw out an admission damaging to C——'s case (No. 18). The form of the question assumes that it would be necessary to hang the child with criminal tendencies when he grows up, which would, of course, be denied by C——. The answer of either "Yes" or "No" to this question involves the acceptance of this assumption.

[61] Opposing P——'s extreme statement that criminal heredity always makes criminals with the equally extreme and equally untrue statement that it plays no part, but that poverty alone makes criminals. Again equivalent to the error of omitting "some" and implying "all" (No. 2).

Note too that C—— has made a considerable shift of the ground of debate (No. 6), now putting forward poverty (*i.e.* environmental conditions) instead of free will in opposition to P——'s insistence on heredity. In fact the determination of conduct by environment has just the same difficulties for a theory of free will as has its determination by heredity, so we must conclude that C—— holds two sets of opinions on the subject which, while not necessarily inconsistent with one another, have not had their mutual implications thought out.

[62] Repeating three times in different words the statement about heredity and poverty (No. 12).

P. If you destroy poverty, the problem will remain exactly the same.[63] Look at the rich criminals.[64] All the modern scientific work on heredity proves the importance of hereditary factors in determining the behavior of the individual.[65]

C. All the best modern philosophy is agreed in stressing the importance of the individual's free will.[66]

[63] Again asserting the extreme and untrue opposite of C——'s proposition. The truth is that there is a positive association between criminality and both criminal heredity and poverty. P—— and C—— seem each equally incapable of thinking in terms of a tendency for B to follow from A (Chapter Two), so make either the extreme and untrue statement that all A is B or that no A is B.

[64] An inconsequent argument (No. 7) if it is intended as a proof of the preceding statement although it is a sound disproof of C——'s statement. The fact that some criminals are not poor is not a proof that there is no tendency for poverty to produce criminality, although it is a disproof of the statement that poverty is the sole cause of crime.

[65] Another diversion from an extreme to a moderate position. What he now says is unquestionably true, but it is not what he said before. Instead of leading inevitably to crime, heredity is now "an important factor."

[66] Another inconsequent argument (No. 7). The statement that free will is important is not a denial of the importance of heredity, although it is put forward as if it were. As is often the case, this inconsequent argument also invites a diversion (No. 6).

In this argument authority is opposed against authority, but with an important difference. P—— is appealing to the general conclusion to be drawn from all biological experiment and observation. C——, on the other hand, is appealing to the "best" philosophy. Even if P—— were willing to admit that the philosophers had a method of establishing this conclusion of equal validity with that of the scientists, he would be suspicious of an appeal to the "best" philosophers. This means that the philosophers whose authority is to be considered are to be selected.

P. Philosophy is said to be the handmaid of theology, and I have no doubt that philosophers are able to find excellent reasons for a conception so useful to theology as free will.[67] For myself, I am more impressed by the fact that science rejects the conception.[68]

I should be interested to know how philosophers have managed to disprove a conclusion so soundly established experimentally as that of the importance of heredity.[69]

C. I can hardly hope to give an account of the present position of free will in philosophy without taking some time over it. With our host's permission I

Their opinions on free will will pretty certainly be one of the marks by which it will be decided whether they belong to the class of the "best philosophers." C——'s appeal to authority is thus also a proof by selected instances (No. 3).

[67] Argument by the imputation of motives (No. 34). P—— is implying that philosophers believe in free will because they need the doctrine for theological purposes. C—— might just as well retort by suggesting that scientists believe in heredity because they want to escape responsibility for their sins.

[68] Makes an appeal to science in the form of an appeal to mere authority (No. 19), as C—— did to the best philosophers. The word "science" is here used vaguely (No. 29), and protects the argument in the same way as C——'s word "best." It is individual scientists and not science that give opinions on free will. Some of these have one opinion, some another. Some of the reasons they give for their opinions are good and some bad. The value of their opinions must be judged by the soundness of their reasons. It cannot be made a matter of appeal to their reasonable authority, since they have no better way of finding out the truth on this matter than the rest of us.

[69] Deals with C——'s inconsequent argument by asking for explanation as to how the conclusions of philosophers affect the question of heredity.

[197]

will do my best. I am afraid this will not be of much interest to you, B——.

B. Well, you have been getting a little out of my depth lately. I wonder whether the truth doesn't lie between your ideas and C——'s, and perhaps heredity and a good home play an equal part in deciding whether a young lad will turn into a criminal.[70] But I should be most interested to hear what you have to say about free will, very interested indeed.[71] Let me look at my watch.

Do you know, I really think we ought to be going up to the drawing room. I hope you won't mind putting off the rest of this discussion to another evening. Most interesting. You won't mind, C——.

C. Oh, no, not at all. You have relieved me of a very difficult task. I have found it a very interesting evening, although I am afraid we have not settled any of the great problems we have been discussing.[72]

[70] True enough, although B—— gives no better reason for it than the recommendation of a mean between two extremes (No. 8). For the word "equal" there can be no possible justification except this argument.

[71] B—— re-enforces this improbable statement by saying it three times (No. 12).

[72] With this statement at any rate we can find ourselves in complete agreement.

Imaginary Discussion on Peace and War Between a Man and a Woman

[The people discussing happen to be British but most of the arguments might equally well be used by Americans. It may be easier to see the weak points in the argument since it is British and not American pacifism and militarism that are being attacked and defended.]

WOMAN: I believe that any country is heading for destruction if it spends its wealth on tanks and airplanes instead of on providing decent homes for its people.

MAN: Well, Margery, if you think that the job of a government is to act as a benevolent grandmother to its incompetents, you should have no quarrel with Great Britain. A country that spends half its revenue on the so-called social service, while . . .[1]

---

[1] Notice the use of emotionally colored phrases. "Providing decent homes" has the same factual meaning as "act as a benevolent grandmother" and as spending on "so-called social service" but arouses the opposite emotional attitude. "Grand-

WOMAN: Nonsense, my dear Ralph, you haven't read the income-tax form you got yesterday. It says there that out of eight hundred and sixty-three million pounds spent altogether, just two hundred and twenty-four million goes to debt payments and over forty million to war pensions. That is what our past wars are costing us. Then there is nearly two hundred and one million for the Army, Navy, and Air Force, to say nothing of an additional eighty million to be raised by borrowing. That is the cost of preparations for the next war. Over five hundred million for wars, past and future. That is the cost of financing imperialist aggression, against only seventy-four million for education, health, and housing together. Where is your half of the revenue spent on social services? [2]

MAN: I have my income-tax form in my pocket.

mother" and "incompetent" are strongly emotionally toned; the first suggesting fussy but unintelligent benevolence, while "incompetents" is used instead of "unemployed" because of the emotional value of its suggestion of moral blame. "So-called" has no factual meaning in the last sentence. Its purpose is merely to call up a vague attitude of disapproval.

[2] This is, in its general outline, a sound argument. Ralph, in saying that more than half of the national revenue was spent on social services, was making a misstatement of fact. In detail, Margery's argument is not so good, since she selects her evidence and is, therefore, guilty of special pleading, as Ralph points out later. The case against Ralph's statement of "more than half of the national revenue" would have been conclusive without any special pleading. The argument illustrates one sound way in which argument can be used to alter the opinions of an opponent—by telling him a fact he didn't know or had forgotten. Also here Margery uses an emotionally colored phrase "financing imperialist aggression." Ralph would probably have called it the cost of "defending democracy against aggression."

Here we are. I thought so; your figures are wrong. Education, health, and housing are not the only social services. You have left out three and a half million for special areas, four and a half million for unemployment grants, forty-six million for old-age pensions, and ninety-six million for health insurance. So your attempt to prove your case by arithmetic is no good.[3]

Anyway, it is not arithmetic that matters here. If you read your income tax form carefully, you would see that the two hundred million pounds are for the *defense* forces. For defense, not aggression. None of our expenditure on the Army and Navy is a threat against anyone; it is for defending our own country and our homes against foreign aggression.[4]

WOMAN: And also for defending the large part of the earth's surface which we have grabbed as our

[3] These figures are correct so the argument is sound against the amounts quoted by Margery. She has clearly selected figures favorable to her case which is what is meant by "special pleading." This, however, is not particularly important since even the correct figures do not support the statement that more than half the revenue is spent on social services. Ralph's last sentence suggests that Margery's omissions refute her whole argument, that is, that his victory on a minor point is equivalent to a victory for his original statement. This is crooked argument by "diversion to a side issue." As proof of Margery's special pleading, Ralph might also have pointed out that she added £80,000,000 borrowed on to the cost of defense without adding it on to the total.

[4] Avoiding the necessity for admitting that he was wrong on the "half its revenue" issue by "diversion" to another question. He cannot, however, be much blamed for this since the diversion was invited by his opponent when she referred to the "cost of financing imperialist aggression."

Empire from the other countries that would like to share it.

MAN: Yes, for that too. I am old-fashioned enough to believe that we have a right to defend our Empire. That is defense, not aggression.[5]

WOMAN: If it is, it is defense of what we have won by aggression in the past.

MAN: Suppose you are right? What do you want to do about it? Do you want us to lay down our arms and let Germany, Italy, and Japan share up India and the rest of our Empire? [6]

WOMAN: I am opposed to all wars; to wars of defense as well as to wars of aggression. If we want to keep our Empire, I believe we shall have to fight for it. If we lose that war, the British Empire will go

---

[5] Emotionally colored words and phrases are used too often to notice them separately. Ralph's "foreign" in the phrase "foreign aggression" has an emotional implication of disapproval absent from Margery's "other countries." "Grabbed from other countries" is a phrase calling up moral disapproval by suggesting the activity of a burglar or pickpocket. Much of the argument is carried on by means of the emotional implications of the words "defense" and "aggression." There is, no doubt, a factual difference between defensive and aggressive wars but the line between them is indefinite and the distinction is difficult to make in practice. Much more important to the argument is the difference between the emotional attitudes aroused by the ideas of defense and aggression.

[6] A good argument. If Margery attacks military preparation, she must be prepared to defend a practicable alternative policy. There are, no doubt, possible answers to Ralph's question, but she is not prepared with one. Finding herself hard pressed she makes a "diversion"; instead of answering Ralph's question, she starts talking about something else—the danger of a war causing the destruction of civilization.

[202]

up in smoke. If we win it, I don't believe we shall be any better off. A big European war, whether we won it or lost it, would destroy the whole fabric of civilization. If civilization blew up, the British Empire would blow up along with it. Isn't it madness to prepare for a war that would wreck us however it finished.[7]

MAN: I agree with you about aggressive wars, and I believe every responsible statesman in our country feels the same. But it is sheer sentimentality to deny us the right to defend our own legitimate interests. If you deny the right of nations to use force in defense of justice, you ought logically to deny the right of society to employ policemen to lock up thieves.[8]

[7] This also is a good argument in itself although it is not an answer to the question that has just been asked. If the point that she urges is correct (that a successful war would destroy the British Empire as well as an unsuccessful one), this fact is obviously one which must be taken into account in considering whether expenditure on armaments can be justified by its necessity for protecting the British Empire. The fact is asserted and not proved. Ralph does not, however, challenge her to prove it. He is probably not altogether easy in his own mind as to whether it is war itself or defeat in war that is the greater danger, so he evades the issue by making another diversion.

We may notice that a principal reason why this discussion reaches no conclusion is because both parties evade every hard point by making a diversion. That is probably the main thing wrong with most arguments. If a discussion is to settle anything, we must resolutely bring our opponent back to the point every time he tries to make a diversion, and, of course, be careful to make no diversions ourselves.

[8] This is a typical "extension." Margery has been arguing against war; Ralph treats her argument as if it were against

[203]

WOMAN: I do deny the right of society to lock up thieves.[9] We have to use force against thieves only because we live in a social system founded on injustice. Instead of distributing the wealth of the world to everybody, we allow a few rich people to keep more than their share and then we have to employ policemen to protect them from the others who haven't got enough.

MAN: But, my dear Margery, you know perfectly well that all crime is not caused by the bad distribution of wealth. In your ideal society founded on social justice, would you deny policemen the right to lock up the murderer of an innocent child? [10]

all use of force. Reference to "logic" is a common trick to introduce the extension. None of us likes to be suspected of being illogical. There is, of course, no logical necessity for Margery to accept Ralph's proposition about policemen and thieves, unless she had said that war is wrong because all use of force is wrong. Whether she thinks this or not, she has not said so yet. She may equally well hold the more moderate position that not all use of force is wrong but that war is a particular use of force which is wrong. Ralph himself would probably disapprove of dueling without believing that all use of force was wrong.

[9] Instead of reaffirming the more moderate statement that war is wrong which is all that is essential to her argument, Margery accepts the extension, which leads her to considerations about social justice which, although important in themselves, have nothing to do with the argument in hand (she is not arguing that social injustice causes war).

[10] The introduction of "innocent children" into an argument is generally to be deplored as tending to deflect judgment by the introduction of irrelevant emotional attitudes. Murdered persons are of all kinds: innocent children, innocent middle-aged men and women, gangsters, wives, and prostitutes. In all cases the murderers are locked up and generally executed if

[204]

WOMAN: I suppose not.[11] There are some crimes, of course, against which one must use force. All the same, I don't see that that has much to do with the question of war.[12]

MAN: It has everything to do with the question of war. A defensive war is simply the way in which international society protects itself against wrong-

they are caught. Innocent children are rather exceptional victims of murder, and such murders have no particular relevance to Ralph's argument. If he had asked, "Would you deny policemen the right to lock up a murderer?" he would have made his point without influencing the answer by irrelevant emotion.

Apart from this, the argument is good. The trap into which Margery fell by accepting Ralph's extension here shuts.

[11] Admitting defeat on this point. It is possible that this defeat is due to Ralph's use of the extension having trapped her into a general condemnation of force which was not her real opinion. It is possible, however, that she did really believe that all use of force was wrong and that it was right for policemen to lock up murderers. To reveal inconsistencies in one's opponent's opinions and to force him to make his decision between them is probably the most important way in which argument can be used to influence opinion. All of us have in our minds opinions that are inconsistent with one another. We may be quite willing to state at one time that all birds fly, and at another time that the ostrich is a bird that does not fly. Inconsistent opinions remain in our minds because they have never been brought face to face with one another. In fact, when such inconsistencies belong to important systems of thought (such as religion and politics) our minds actively resist any attempt to bring them face to face and the inconsistencies may remain until we die. It is a great value of discussion with other people that it may force us to face these inconsistencies and to make the choice between them which we should have evaded if we had been left to ourselves.

[12] Nothing, of course, unless one admits that condemnation of war implies condemnation of all use of force. Unfortunately for her, Margery has accepted that view.

doers. The British defense forces are the world's policeman.[13] The trouble with you, Margery, is that you seem to be able to think clearly enough about other things, but you feel so strongly about war that it makes you all muddled and inconsistent. That is the trouble with you pacifists. In that book you lent me last week, I noticed it said that in the defense of Madrid a group of Oxford pacifists distinguished themselves by their efficiency in handling machine guns. How is that for inconsistency in men who believe that all use of force is wrong.[14]

[13] An argument from analogy. Not a good argument since Margery might have pointed out that a little earlier Ralph had referred to the function of the armed forces as "to defend our own legitimate interests" and that it is not the function of a policeman to defend his own legitimate interests. Obviously one can argue in favor of the right of a nation to defend its own interests but not by using the analogy of a policeman.

[14] Obviously there is an inconsistency somewhere, but it may not be in the alleged Oxford machine gunners. Presumably the pacifists who believe that all use of force is wrong are not the same pacifists as use machine guns. If this is the case, the inconsistency is not in the machine gunners but in the use of the word "pacifist." The word seems to be used in three senses: (a) for one who believes that all use of force is wrong, (b) for one who believes that all war is wrong, and (c) for one who dislikes military domination and is willing to fight against it. The machine gunners would be inconsistent if they were pacifists in sense (a) or (b) but not if they were pacifists in sense (c). It is, of course, arguable that this is not a right sense in which to use the word "pacifist" but it is often so used, and it is obviously in this sense that the machine gunners are called pacifists. To avoid confusion due to ambiguities in the meanings of words, it is not a bad idea to follow the old rule of defining the terms you use in argument. An opponent who is always asking you to define your terms is often merely a nuisance, but sometimes (as here) he would be justified.

WOMAN: I think, of course, that pacifists using machine guns are wrong, but you, at least, Ralph, ought to recognize the heroism of men who are ready to sacrifice their lives for an idea, even if you think that idea is mistaken.[15] But all this sacrifice of life in Spain and in China is dreadful. I want it to stop. How can you maintain that war is a good thing?

MAN: I am not prepared to say that war is a good thing.[16] I know that it is a necessary thing. Men always have fought wars and always will. Man is a fighting animal. He has an instinct to fight. You can't change human nature.[17]

WOMAN: You shoot, don't you? Shoot birds, I mean.

MAN: I do. What's that got to do with it?

WOMAN: Suppose a keeper found a poacher on your moor, and suppose the poacher said that man was a hunting animal, that he had a hunting instinct, and that human nature couldn't be changed. Would you let him off?

MAN: Of course not. I should hand him over to a

[15] Instead of pointing out the real weakness in Ralph's argument, Margery again makes a diversion. Obviously if a man is charged with being inconsistent, it is no defense against that charge to say that he is heroic. It is a mere diversion of the argument to another topic.

[16] Margery's last remark was another example of the dishonest device of the extension. Ralph had not said that war was a good thing. More wily in debating than Margery, he does not fall into the trap. He here makes the correct response of refusing to accept the extension and of affirming instead the more moderate statement which he is prepared to defend.

[17] Using the oratorical trick of repeated affirmation. Using different words, he has made the same statement four times.

policeman. That is what the police are for. I should hope that a dose of imprisonment would cure his enthusiasm for hunting my birds.

WOMAN: So you believe that human nature can be changed by imprisonment. And you don't believe that men always have to go on doing what their instincts drive them to.[18] Who's being muddleheaded and inconsistent now?

MAN: I am not inconsistent. What I said and what I still maintain is that I have a right to defend my own legitimate interests, and that nations have a right to defend their own legitimate interests.[19]

What's the good of arguing? We shall never agree on this subject. Let's have a swim.

WOMAN: O.K. Ralph, I'd rather swim than argue.[20]

[18] A sound argument of the same general character as one previously used by Ralph. Margery discovers that he has other opinions inconsistent with the general principle which he has laid down as an argument for the necessity of war: the unchangeableness of "human instincts." She has not proved that he was wrong before, but simply that either he was wrong before or he is wrong now. He must make his choice between keeping his general principle and applying it both to war and poaching, or of giving it up. Those who remember Plato will recognize this as the essential method of the Socratic dialogues.

[19] Hard pressed, Ralph, as usual, makes a diversion. This time, it is to an earlier point in the argument.

[20] A wise decision. All the same, something has come out of the argument. Ralph is probably convinced that Great Britain does not spend more than half its revenue on social services. Margery has had it demonstrated to her that she does not believe that all use of force is wrong so she cannot use that argument against war. Ralph has similarly been deprived of his argument that war is necessary because human instincts cannot change (unless he is willing to stop prosecuting poachers which, we can safely assume, he is not).

Reasoning Tests

INSTRUCTIONS for carrying out the reasoning tests. You will find in the pages following three tests of reasoning ability marked A, B, and C. A is an easy one. B and C are both equally difficult and are both harder than A. B and C can be used at different times by the same person. Test B, for example, may be used before reading the book, and Test C after reading the book. A comparison of one's scores can thus be made, indicating roughly whether improvement in logical reasoning has taken place. Test A may be used for practice before going on to B or C by those for whom A is too easy as a test.

In each test there are a number of arguments, followed by a *conclusion* in italics. There are twelve arguments in Test A and sixteen in each of Tests B and C. The instructions for doing Tests A, B, and C are exactly the same, so also are the methods of marking.

You are first asked to read through each of the *conclusions* in the test you are doing (that is, to read the part printed in italics) without bothering about the rest of the argument. If you think that the conclusion is true, put a ring round the word "true"; if

you think it is false, put a ring round the word "false";
if you have no opinion as to whether it is true or false,
put a ring round the "?"

For example, the argument might be:

(M) True All fishes breathe under water,

?   but whales have to come up to the Sound

     air in order to breathe, so we

False know that *whales are not fishes*. Unsound

Most of us (unlike the author of *Moby Dick*)
will probably agree with this conclusion. We should,
therefore, put a ring round the word "true." When
this has been done for all the arguments in the test
(and not before), pass on to the second part of the
test. Any marks you have made can be altered if you
wish, while you are still doing the first part of the
test, but they must not be altered after the second
part of the test has been started.

For the second part of the test, read each of the
arguments in full and consider whether it is a sound
or an unsound argument. Read the argument through
as often as you need to come to a decision. An argument is sound if the conclusion follows necessarily
from the statements that have gone before it (the
premises). If the conclusion does not necessarily follow from the premises (which you are to accept as
being true), the argument is unsound whether or not
the conclusion is in itself a true one. If you consider
that any particular argument is sound, put a ring
around the word "sound"; if you consider that the
argument is unsound, put a ring around the word "unsound."

[210]

Thus the argument already given is sound since, if it is true that *all* fishes breathe under water and that whales do not, it must necessarily follow that whales are not fishes. The word "sound" should therefore be circled for this argument.

Let us suppose that the argument had run:

(N) True   All fishes breathe under water,   Sound
    ?   and carp breathe under water, so
  False   *carp are fishes*.   Unsound

It would now be necessary to circle the word "unsound" because, though the conclusion happens to be true, it does not follow necessarily from the premises. Clearly it does not, because it has not been stated that *all* animals which breathe under water are fishes. In fact, there are other animals besides fishes that breathe under water.

Again, the argument might have run

(O) True   All fishes breathe under water,   Sound
    ?   and tadpoles breathe under water,
  False so *tadpoles are fishes*.   Unsound

It would then be an unsound argument (because the premises do not say that *only* fishes breathe under water), supporting a false conclusion. Both the above arguments, (N) and (O), are equally unsound because the conclusion does not follow necessarily from what has gone before. One may assert a conclusion which is, in itself, true, even though the reasoning to that conclusion is illogical and unsound, as in (N). In like fashion, we have observed that it is possible

to come to an untrue conclusion by starting with untrue premises, even though the reasoning from these
premises is sound, as in (M).

In the tests themselves, some of the premises are
true, some are false, and some are matters of opinion.
You are not asked to express any opinion as to their
truth or falsity. In each argument there are two
premises, though in the harder tests they may not be
clearly divided. You must treat both as if they were
true and ask whether, if they were true, the conclusion would necessarily follow. If it would, the argument is sound; if it would not, the argument is unsound.

There are no catches in these tests. The words used
mean what they seem to mean. If the same phrase is
used twice in the argument, it means the same thing
each time, and if two different forms of words which
seem to have the same meaning are used in two places
in the argument, you can take it that they really do
have the same meanings.

To sum up:

First, go through the conclusion only of each argument and put a ring around the word "true" if you
think it is true, around the word "false" if you think
it is false, and around the "?" if you have no opinion
as to its truth or falsity. You can make any altera-
tions you like in these marks while you are doing this
part of the test, but not after the next part of the test
is started.

Secondly, go through each of the arguments in full
and ask yourself whether, if the preceding part of

the argument were true, the conclusion would necessarily follow. If it would, put a circle around the word "sound"; if it would not, put a circle around the word "unsound."

If you do not want to mark your copies of the test, there is, of course, no reason why you should not copy the numbers of the arguments on to a sheet of paper and write "T" after the number for a true conclusion, "F" for a false one, etc. This will not take much longer.

Test A

Easy Test of Reasoning

(12 questions)

Do not start reading this test until you have read the instructions on pages 209–213.

(1) True — Every Russian is an idealist at heart. All Bolsheviks are Russians, so we may be sure that *every Bolshevik is an idealist at heart*. — Sound / Unsound

?

False

(2) True — Some Russians are idealists. All Bolsheviks are Russians. It follows, therefore, that *some Bolsheviks are idealists*. — Sound / Unsound

?

False

(3) True — Every Russian is an idealist. All Bolsheviks are idealists. Therefore, *some Bolsheviks are Russians*. — Sound / Unsound

?

False

(4) True — No Bolsheviks are idealists and all Bolsheviks are Russians. Therefore, *some Russians are not idealists*. — Sound / Unsound

?

False

(5) True — Some sailors are not able to swim. All Nantucketers can swim. Therefore, *no Nantucketers are sailors*. — Sound / Unsound

?

False

(6) True — The Eskimos are the only people who eat nothing but meat and — Sound

[214]

?   it is found that all Eskimos have good teeth. So we may conclude   **Unsound**
False   that *no people who eat only meat have bad teeth.*

(7) True   Many brightly colored snakes are poisonous. The copperhead   **Sound**
?   snake is not brightly colored. So *the copperhead is not a poisonous*   **Unsound**
False   *snake.*

(8) True   All poets die young but many professors are old, so we may con-   **Sound**
?   clude that *not all professors are*
False   *poets.*   **Unsound**

(9) True   There is no doubt that some drugs are harmful. All alcoholic   **Sound**
?   liquors contain the drug alcohol. Therefore, *some alcoholic liquors*   **Unsound**
False   *are harmful.*

(10) True   No peace settlement is satis-factory to both sides. The only   **Sound**
?   lasting settlements are those which satisfy both sides. There-   **Unsound**
False   fore, *no peace settlement is last-ing.*

(11) True   There are some fevers that are not dangerous. No colds are dan-   **Sound**
?   gerous. Therefore, *some colds are*
False   *not fevers.*   **Unsound**

(12) True   All poisonous things are bitter.   **Sound**
?   Arsenic is not bitter. Therefore,
False   *arsenic is not poisonous.*   **Unsound**

[The key to Test A will be found on page 232]

Test B

Advanced Test of Reasoning

(16 questions)

(13) True
?
False

At the time of General Franco's rebellion, the Spanish government had Communists among its members. It is not to be doubted that any government with Communist members is under the influence of Moscow. So General Franco was justified in his assertion that *the Spanish government at the time of the rebellion was under Moscow's influence.*

Sound

Unsound

(14) True
?
False

It should be a central principle of American politics to avoid any policy which may land this country in a war which is not in defense of our own vital interests. Any entanglement in European international politics will lead to the necessity for fighting wars in which no essential American interest is at stake. So *America ought to avoid any commitments in European international affairs.*

Sound

Unsound

(15) True

A wider and fairer distribution of social products is one of the dis-

Sound

? tinctive aims of socialism. It is, however, also an ideal at which capitalism aims and which it has done a great deal to achieve. We see, therefore, that *it is a mistake to suppose that there is any conflict between the aims of socialism and of capitalism.*

False

Unsound

(16) True   Many people fear that the prosperity of American industry may decline under increasing government control. They should remember, however, that the tariff system is itself a form of government control of industry and that our industries have prospered as a result of this system. This shows that *government control is never harmful to industry.*

?

False

Sound

Unsound

(17) True   Every woman is a potential mother, and no one possessing this sacred potentiality is capable of committing crimes of the worst kind. It follows from this that *none of the worst criminals are women.*

?

False

Sound

Unsound

(18) True   No one has ever done any harm to his health by moderate indulgence in a mild drug. Nicotine is a mild drug and few cigarette smokers can afford to smoke excessively. So *it is nonsense to suppose that cigarette smoking ever does any harm to health.*

?

False

Sound

Unsound

[217]

(19) True   A man is ennobled by the ex-
            perience of finding himself faced   Sound
     ?   by the choice between life and
            death. War provides the supreme   Unsound
  False   situation in which men have to
            make this choice, so that, *if uni-*
            versal and perpetual peace could
            be attained, it would be at the
            price of robbing men of all en-
            nobling experience.

(20) True   Any government is justified in
            taking any measures it may con-   Sound
     ?   sider necessary to repress its ene-
            mies. The German Jews are ene-   Unsound
  False   mies of the Nazi government. So
            the Nazi repression of the Jews
            is justified.

(21) True   One of the forms of preparation
            for war in which we are expected
     ?   to engage is the taking of de-   Sound
            fensive measures against the pos-
  False   sibility of air attack. But if we   Unsound
            believe that all warfare is wrong
            and that all preparations for war
            are wrong, we must admit that *it*
            is not right to take part in de-
            fensive measures against air at-
            tack.

(22) True   Only those with healthy bodies
            and with healthy minds are truly   Sound
     ?   healthy. From this we see that *a*
            healthy body is a necessary con-   Unsound
  False   *dition for a healthy mind.*

[218]

(23) True   The more a policeman knows, the more efficient he becomes. No man can take a university degree without learning more than he would have known otherwise. So *a policeman will become more efficient if he takes a university degree.*

    ?

    False

Sound

Unsound

(24) True   American enterprises cannot develop profitably in China unless China's own resources are developed. The conquest of China by Japan would result in the speedy development of China's resources. Therefore, *the Japanese conquest of China would be of profit to American enterprises in China.*

    ?

    False

Sound

Unsound

(25) True   An aerial bomb that has fallen somewhere not in the neighborhood of some military objective must have been dropped with the deliberate intention of causing injury to civilians. Undoubtedly there have been many bombardments in Spain by the airplanes of General Franco in which bombs have fallen in places where there were no military objectives. So *it must be concluded that General Franco's aviators have dropped bombs intended to injure civilians.*

    ?

    False

Sound

Unsound

(26) True   One major factor which must be taken into account in consider-

Sound

?   ing the transference of territory
                 from one country to another is   Unsound
False   the wishes of the majority of the
                 inhabitants of the territory in
                 question. There is no doubt that
                 the majority of the inhabitants
                 of the Sudeten districts wished
                 their territory to be transferred
                 from Czechoslovakia to Germany.
                 Therefore, *it was right that the
                 transfer of the Sudeten districts
                 from Czechoslovakia to Germany
                 should have taken place.*

(27) True   The invasion of Great Britain
                 by the Romans and of America   Sound
?   by European settlers were exam-
                 ples of invasions of culturally   Unsound
False   backward areas by more civilized
                 peoples which resulted ultimately
                 in benefit to the countries in-
                 vaded. Abyssinia was also a cul-
                 turally backward area which was
                 invaded by the more civilized
                 Italians. Therefore, *the invasion
                 of Abyssinia by Italy must ulti-
                 mately benefit Abyssinia.*

(28) True   No legal system is sound which
                 ignores the facts of life. One of   Sound
?   the facts of life at the present day
                 in America is the undermining of   Unsound
False   states' rights by the far-spread
                 corporate ownership of power, in-
                 dustry and business. So *if our
                 legal system is sound, it must
                 take into account the undermin-*

[220]

ing of states' rights which results from present tendencies of industrial development.

[The key to Test B will be found on page 234]

Test C

Advanced Test of Reasoning

(16 questions)

(29) True

?

False

However ardently we may believe in freedom, we must admit
the right and duty of every country to limit the freedom of its
citizens to do anything that is
harmful to themselves. It must
also be admitted that the drinking of wines and spirits is always,
to some degree, harmful. It follows that *we must admit the right-
ness of the total prohibition by
law of the drinking of wines and
spirits.*

Sound

Unsound

(30) True

?

False

Social harm always results
from going against biological
principles. There is no more fun-
damental biological principle than
that which prohibits marriage between people of different races,
so *we cannot regard marriage between white Americans and Negroes as socially desirable.*

Sound

Unsound

(31) True

?

There is no better sign that a
man's health is good than the fact
that he lives to a great age. It is
a fact that if we examine the life

Sound

Unsound

[222]

False records of vegetarians, we find that some of them live to a great age. We can conclude from this that *a sound rule for health is to give up the eating of meat.*

(32) True
?
False

Among the most precious of the personal liberties conferred on the citizen of the democratic state is the power to control, criticize, and change the government. The citizens of the United States have not lost these privileges under the New Deal. So *the personal liberty of the American citizen has not been reduced under the New Deal.*

Sound

Unsound

(33) True
?
False

There is no satisfactory way of dealing with a socially harmful form of trading except that of clapping on taxes until it is forced out of existence. There is no doubt that the chain stores are harmful to the producers, to their own employees, and ultimately to the purchasers. Therefore, *the chain stores should be taxed out of existence.*

Sound

Unsound

(34) True
?
False

It is found that houses in which a dog is kept are never visited by burglars. It is also found that houses with telephones are seldom visited by burglars. So it follows that *some houses in which a dog is kept are fitted with telephones.*

Sound

Unsound

[223]

(35) True   It is always murder to kill another person and all murder is   Sound
?   morally wrong. Therefore, *it can never be morally right to kill an*   Unsound
False   *incurable invalid even if he consents.*

(36) True   No social activity can properly be called "great" unless it serves   Sound
?   some moral purpose. Poetry is a kind of social activity which may   Unsound
False   or may not have a moral end. From which we may conclude that *all great poetry, properly so called, serves some moral purpose.*

(37) True   No man can be blamed for destroying anything that belongs   Sound
?   to himself. The life that he destroys by suicide belongs to himself   Unsound
False   self alone. Therefore, *suicide is an act for which no man can be blamed.*

(38) True   No man can be blamed for any characteristic with which he was   Sound
?   born or for any consequence of such a characteristic. Some men   Unsound
False   are criminals because they were born with criminal characteristics. So it follows that *some criminals are not to be blamed for being criminals.*

(39) True   Slavery was an inefficient form of labor because of the lack of   Sound
?   incentive to individual effort. A similar lack of incentive is an in-   Unsound

False   evitable consequence of communism or socialism. So *communism
and socialism are, in effect, forms
of slavery.*

(40) True   We must admit that the occur-
rence of quintuplets is an unusual   Sound
?   event, but, to excite the legitimate
interest of a reasonable person, it   Unsound
False   is not sufficient that an event
should be merely unusual. So *no
reasonable person should be interested in the Dionne quintuplets.*

(41) True   It is claimed that Fascism has
brought prosperity to the coun-   Sound
?   tries that have adopted it. But
there are thousands who are wait-   Unsound
False   ing to emigrate from Germany
when they get the chance. We
may be sure that no one would
wish to emigrate from a prosper-
ous country, so we may conclude
that *any stories we may hear of
the prosperity of a Fascist country are mythical.*

(42) True   All true Americans have a
marked sense of humor. This   Sound
?   sense of humor is noticeably lack-
ing in all Communists. So *no true*   Unsound
False   *American can be a Communist.*

(43) True   All good painting obeys the
laws of perspective. Most of the   Sound
?   painting of Chinese and Japanese artists disregards these laws.   Unsound

[225]

False   Therefore, *none of the paintings of Japanese or Chinese artists is of the highest rank.*

(44) True   Whenever we meet a man without personal ambition, we   Sound

?   find that he is free from that arrogance of manner which is an   Unsound

False   unpleasant characteristic of some successful people. Some of the dictators also show this delightful characteristic of freedom from arrogance. So we may be sure that *some dictators are without personal ambition.*

[The key to Test C will be found on page 236]

RULES FOR SCORING THE TESTS

The first part of each of the tests (in which conclusions were marked as true or false) was not intended as a test of reasoning; it was merely an expression of opinion. These "true" and "false" marks will be used later, but for the present purpose of measuring reasoning ability they may be ignored.

In order to mark the tests for reasoning ability, refer to the keys for the tests (page 232 for Test A, page 234 for Test B, and page 236 for Test C). On each test, give yourself two points for every time that you have correctly marked an argument as "sound" or "unsound," and total these points.

This total will not do as the test score because, if you have no reasoning power and merely guess the answers to all the questions, you are likely to get half right by chance alone, which would give you the misleading total of 12 for Test A and 16 for the other two tests, even if you had no ability at all to do the tests correctly.

Subtract, therefore, from the total already obtained one point for each of the questions which you have answered, whether the answer was right or wrong (*i.e.*, the score you would have been likely to get by chance alone). No points are to be deducted for any question which you have not marked either "sound"

[227]

or "unsound." The quantity which you have left is your score for the test. If you want a permanent record of this, a form is provided for entering it with your name on page 238. The maximum score is 12 for Test A and 16 for each of the other two tests. When we use this method of scoring it is possible by chance for a bad scorer to get less than zero. If you are so unfortunate as to get such a score, enter it as zero.

We now come to the use of the "true" and "false" marks. These are intended to measure how far your judgment of the soundness or unsoundness of an argument is affected by your opinions as to the truth of the conclusions—that is, how far your reasoning is influenced by your prejudices. If your opinions as to the truth or falsity of the conclusions were influencing your judgment as to the soundness or unsoundness of the argument, you would be more inclined to mark as "sound" the arguments which have been marked "true" and also more inclined to mark as "unsound" the arguments that you have marked "false." In other words, amongst the arguments you have marked as "true," the mistakes made will generally be in marking as "sound" the arguments that are really unsound, while amongst the arguments you have marked as "false," any mistakes are likely to be mostly of the opposite kind—really sound arguments which have been marked as "unsound."

The first step is to count how many mistakes have been made in which either an argument marked as "true" has been marked as "sound" when it should have been "unsound" or an argument marked "false" has been marked "unsound" when it should have been sound. This number may be called A.

Second, count how many times you have avoided making this kind of mistake, that is, the number of right answers which are marked either as "true" and "unsound" or as "false" and "sound." This number may be called B.

Third, count how many mistakes are of the kind opposite to those counted before, that is, the number of times that either an argument marked as "true" has been marked "unsound" when it should have been "sound," or an argument marked as "false" has been marked "sound" when it should have been "unsound." This number may be called C.

Fourth, count how many times you have avoided making this last kind of mistake, that is, the number of right answers which are marked either as "true" and "sound" or as "false" and "unsound." This number may be called D.

Arguments in which the "?" has been circled instead of the "true" or "false" are not counted at all for the present purpose. Nor are those (if any) in which neither "sound" nor "unsound" has been circled.

Now, A is the number of times you have made a mistake in line with your personal opinions or prejudices, while B is the number of times you have avoided making this kind of mistake. In the same way, C is the number of times you have made a mistake which goes against your prejudices, while D is the number of times you have avoided making this kind of mistake.

If your judgments of "sound" and "unsound" were not affected at all by your opinion as to whether the conclusion was true or false, we should expect that the fraction A/B would be equal to C/D, that is, that mistakes of the first kind would be as likely as mistakes of the second kind. If, on the other hand, your judgments of soundness were affected by your opinions about the truth of the conclusion, we should expect that mistakes of the first kind would happen on a greater proportion of the cases than would mistakes of the second kind. A/B would then be greater than C/D.

In order to get a measure of your impartiality, it is, therefore, necessary to calculate some quantity which measures how closely A/B and C/D are the same.

We begin by multiplying A by D and B by C. Let us call these two quantities X and Y. Now if A/B is the same as C/D, it follows that X and Y will also be equal, whereas if A/B is greater than C/D, X will be greater than Y. The effect of prejudice on judgments about soundness is therefore measured by the amount that X is greater than Y; impartiality is shown by X being equal to Y.

We can measure the degree of impartiality by multiplying Y by 20 and dividing the result by the sum of X and Y, expressing the result to the nearest whole number. If you were completely unprejudiced in your judgments of soundness, X would be equal to Y, so this quantity would be 10; if, on the other hand, your opinion as to the soundness of an argument invariably depended on your opinion as to the truth of its conclusion, this quantity would be zero (because B and C, and therefore Y, would be zero).

If all your answers are right, you score 10 for impartiality and there is no need to go through the above calculations. The score for impartiality will generally be most reliable if several mistakes have been made, so that it is possible to judge how important prejudice is as a factor in causing those mistakes. The calculation is a little more complicated than that of getting a measure of reasoning ability. This is necessary because there are more factors to take into account. The arithmetic, however, is not difficult and should offer no obstacle to anyone who is able to do the reasoning test.

Let us suppose that you have marked four answers "true" and "sound," of which 2 are right and 2 are wrong; one right answer of "true" and "unsound"; seven answers of "false" and "unsound" of which 4 are right and 3 wrong; and four of "false" and "sound," of which 2 are right and 2 wrong.

We can show the steps of working out in convenient tabular form:

Step 1. We have counted the number of right and wrong answers of each kind and have got:

	TS	TU	FU	FS
Right	2	1	4	2
Wrong	2	0	3	2

(TS is a convenient contraction for answers that have been marked "true" and "sound," TU for those marked "true" and "unsound," and so on.)

Step. 2   A = TS (wrong) + FU (wrong) = 2 + 3 = 5
            B = TU (right) + FS (right) = 1 + 2 = 3
            C = TU (wrong) + FS (wrong) = 0 + 2 = 2
            D = TS (right) + FU (right) = 2 + 4 = 6

Step 3.   A × D = 5 × 6 = 30   So X = 30
              B × C = 3 × 2 = 6   So Y = 6

Step. 4.   20Y ÷ (X + Y) = 120 ÷ 36 = 3 (to the nearest whole number).

This is a low score for freedom from prejudice. It means that a person obtaining such a score is very much inclined to judge an argument to be sound if he agrees with its conclusion and unsound if he does not.

A score of 10 for impartiality means that your judgments have been completely impartial. It is possible, however, to get a score of more than 10. This indicates that on the given test you have tended more to make a judgment opposed to your prejudices than to make one in line with them. This may be simply accidental in terms of the setup of this particular test, or it may indicate a more general tendency in this direction.

To sum up:

1. To get a measure of reasoning ability. "True," "false," and "?" marks are ignored. Add up the total number of questions correctly marked as "sound" or "unsound," double this number and subtract from it the total number of arguments which have been

marked as "sound" or "unsound," including those wrongly marked.

2. To get a measure of impartiality. All arguments in which "?" has been circled are ignored and so also are all those in which neither "sound" nor "unsound" has been circled. Count up the number wrong and the number right of those that have been marked "true" and "sound," of those that have been marked "true" and "unsound," and so on. Calculate TS (wrong) plus FU (wrong) and call this A; calculate TU (right) plus FS (right) and call this B; calculate TU (wrong) plus FS (wrong) and call this C; and calculate TS (right) plus FU (right) and call this D. Now multiply A by D and call the result X; also multiply B by C and call the result Y. The measure of impartiality is the nearest whole number to 20 times Y divided by $(X + Y)$. The score of 10 indicates complete impartiality.

Key to Test A

(1)	Sound	(7)	Unsound
(2)	Unsound	(8)	Sound
(3)	Unsound	(9)	Unsound
(4)	Sound	(10)	Sound
(5)	Unsound	(11)	Unsound
(6)	Sound	(12)	Sound

REASONING TESTS

Key to Test B

(13) Sound	(21) Sound
(14) Sound	(22) Unsound
(15) Unsound	(23) Sound
(16) Unsound	(24) Unsound
(17) Sound	(25) Sound
(18) Unsound	(26) Unsound
(19) Unsound	(27) Unsound
(20) Sound	(28) Sound

REASONING TESTS

Key to Test C

(29)	Sound	(37)	Sound
(30)	Sound	(38)	Sound
(31)	Unsound	(39)	Unsound
(32)	Unsound	(40)	Unsound
(33)	Sound	(41)	Unsound
(34)	Unsound	(42)	Sound
(35)	Sound	(43)	Unsound
(36)	Sound	(44)	Unsound

Score Sheet for Reasoning Tests

Name	Test	Reasoning Score	Score for Impartiality

Index

INDEX

INDEX

ture examined, 152 ff; origin in childhood emotions, 153-4; in other emotions, 154; its irrational character rationalized, 155; how to offset in making judgments, 155-6; productive of "special pleading," 157; how to deal with this, 159-60;
how exploited by orators, 160-61; by appeal based on practical consequences to hearers, 160; need for detachment in resisting, 162-3; not to be hastily attributed to opponent, 163

prepossessions, appeals to the audience's, 77-9, 160-63, 178, 179

Presidential election (1936), 20-21, 42-4, 60-62

prestige, suggestion by, 58, 61-3, 67, 70-74, *182, 187, 189, 190;* by false credentials, 63, *194;* by use of technical jargon, 63-7; when real, 70-71; how to resist, 69-70, 174-5

proletarian and capitalist, distinction between, 128-9

proof by selected instances—*see* selected instances

property, public *vs* private ownership of, 10, 87

prosperity, national, its real meaning, 109

psychoanalysis, 10

psychology—use of words in, 9-10; of analogy in, 109-110

psychology textbooks—definitions in, 130; examples from, to illustrate clear understanding of words, 135, 138

public works, 158

quack healer's tricks, 62-4, 70, 78

quantum theory, 106

question, form of, dictating answer, 68-9

radicals, 52-3

rationality, "continuous variation" in, 130

rationalization, 154-5, 163

receptivity, audience, 77-8

red-haired people and bad temper, 23-7

relativity, 79-80, 92

relief, attacks on, 160

religion, definition of, 132-3

religions, comparative, study of, 81-2

repeated affirmation, 58-60, 174, *190, 195, 198, 207*

Republican party, 20, 42-3

ridicule, 39, 151-2

Rivers, Dr., 74

Robeson, Paul, 36

Roosevelt, President F. D., 42, 44, 60-61, 166

Roosevelt, Mrs. F. D., 53

Rousseau, J. J., 94

"rugged individualism," 43, 157

Ruskin's criticism of Whistler, 13

Russia—Red and White Armies, 11; treason trials, 27; conditions in, 32, 36-7; working men in, 36,'42; persecution of Christians, 37, 42; Soviet Union, 53; second Revolution, 95

Sacco and Vanzetti, 84

sailing analogy, 116-17

sanity, degrees of, 122-3

Schopenhauer, Arthur, 67

science—use of objective words in books on, 7-9; use of analogy in, 105-108; straight thinking in, 164; its methods applied to practical problems, 165 ff

scientific methods in thinking, 164-5

selected facts as basis of error, 148

selected instances, proof by, 31, 172, *196-7, 200, 201*

Serajevo, assassination at, 83-4

sex, 9, 88, 91

Shakespeare, 99

Shaw, George Bernard, 87, 89, 158

Shelley, P. B., 138

shocked, benefits of being, 86-7

side issues, diversion to, 38-9, 173

simplification of complex ideas impracticable, 91 ff

Sinclair, Upton, 87

slogans, 94-5

Smith, Alfred E., 61

social problems, use of "extension" trick in discussing, 34-5

social sciences—use of analogy in, 108-109; definitions in books on, 130

social security benefits, 158

Socialist party, 42-4

"some A is B"—*see* "all A is B"

INDEX

sophistical formula used for evasion, 35, 36, 173, *185*

Soviet Union—*see* Russia

space-time system, four-dimensional, 106

Spanish Civil War, 11, 84, 98

Spearman, Professor, 9

special pleading, 157-60, 178; examples of, 158-9, *183, 187, 193, 194, 201*

speculative arguments, 143-4, 145, 178, *193*

speculative thinking, 141-6; limitations, 142-3

sport, tendency toward tabloid thinking in, 98

statistical method of combating "all A is B" arguments, 23-6

struggle for existence, 107

suggestion—*see* tricks of suggestion

surtax on incomes, 154

Swinburne, A. C., 5, 21

syllogism with undistributed middle, 47-53

tabloid judgments, 91-102, *183, 185, 192;* inconsistent with truth, 91 ff; how used, 92-4; as slogans, 94-5; explanation of, 95-6; serviceable in wartime, 96-7; in elections, 97-8, 102; in sport, 98; in learning history, 98-9; as a spur to action, 99-100

tariffs, 10, 91

taxation, 68, 91, 148, 154; its effect on our pockets, 160-61

teachers' attitude toward controversy, 73-4

technical language, 40, 63-7, *190;* how to deal with when used to suggest prestige, 175

tests in reasoning procedure, 209-32

textbooks, unnecessary obscurity of, 63

thinking—abstract, 137-40; concrete, 140-41; speculative, 141-6

thought habits, 77-90, *183, 186, 193;* appeal to, 77-8; traditional, 79; close our minds, 81, 88, 90; religious and moral, 81-2; in international questions, 82-6; how shocked, 87; lead to fear of discussing certain questions, 88; how changed, 88-90

traditional beliefs, 73, 79

triangle in Euclidean and non-Euclidean geometries, 80-81, 89

tricks of suggestion, 31-46; selected instances, 31, 172, *196-7, 200, 201;* extension and misrepresentation, 33-5, 92-3, 159, 172, *184, 185, 203-204, 205, 207;* use of sophistical formula for evading a sound refutation, 35, 36, 173, *185;* diversion to another question, 36-7, 173 (*see* diversion); to a side issue, 38; irrelevant objection, 38-9, 50, 173, *117, 151, 173, 188;* by ridicule, 39, 151-2;

substituting a moderate statement, 39-40; inconsequent argument, 40-42, 173, *189, 196;* advocating a mean between two extremes, 42-6, 47, 173, *198;* repeated affirmation, 58-60, 174, *190, 195, 198, 207;* confident manner, 60, 174, *186;* suggesting prestige—*see* prestige; affected failure to understand, 67-8, 175, *190, 191;* form of question dictating answer, 68-9; how to resist this, 69-70; drawing out damaging admissions, 68-9, 175, *195;* appeal to mere authority, 72-3, 175;

use of acceptable statements to compel acceptance of doubtful, 77-8, 175; phrasing doubtful to fit audience's thought habits, 78-9, 160, 176; use of tabloid arguments, 92-9, 176, *183, 185, 192;* refusal to make a decision either way, 99-100, 176;

argument by imperfect analogy, 110-14, 176, *189;* by forced analogy, 114-18, 177; by ignoring "continuous variation," 119-27, 177; by illegitimate demand for definition, 129-31, *191;* ambiguity or vagueness, 132-9, 178; speculative argument, 140-46, 178; angering the opponent, 151-2, 178; special pleading, 157-60, 178, *183, 187, 193, 194, 201;* appeal based on practical consequences to hearer, 160-63, 179, *183, 194;* attributing motives to opponent, 163, 179, *197*

Trotzky, Leon, 44, 53

[246]

INDEX

Trotzkyites, 17, 84
truth of long-accepted beliefs, 73, 79; of the "obvious," 80; of the contradictory or inconceivable, 144-5 (*see also* speculative thinking)

unconscious, the, 135, 145-6
understand, failure to—*see* affected failure to understand
undistributed middle term, 47-53, 92, 173-4
unions—*see* labor unions
unrelated statements, diversion by means of, 36-7, 173

vagueness in terms, 132-9, 178, *182, 187, 190, 197. See also* ambiguity
verifying evidence, 156
voting, 100

war—use of emotional words in, 5-6, 11; arguments about, 5, 11, 68-9; thought habits during, 82-3; benefits of, according to a bishop, 114
Washington, Booker T., 36

wealth, distribution of, 41, 161-2
Whistler criticized by Ruskin, 13
Wilhelm II, Kaiser, 85
wishful thinking, 152-3, 161-2
woman suffrage, 21
women, college degrees for, 35
words—their meanings, 3 ff, 133-4, 136, 178 (*see also* ambiguity); emotional tone in argument, 3-4, 55, 168, 172, *181, 182, 183, 184, 188, 193, 199-200, 202, 204;* in wartime, 5-6, 11; in poetry, 5-7; in science, 7-9, 164; in psychology, 9-10; in discussions of sex, 9-10; of politics and international problems, 10-12, 17-18; of disarmament, 11; in art criticism, 12-13; in literary criticism, 13-16; in criminal trials, 16;
objective use of, 15-16; effect of emotional use of on our private thinking, 18-19; use of in different senses in argument, 133; use of abstract, 134 (*see also* ambiguity)
work, "making" it by construction of battleships, 157-8
World War, 5, 93, 96

[247]

ABOUT THE AUTHOR

ROBERT H. THOULESS *is Professor of Psychology at Glasgow University. He was born at Norwich, England, in 1894 and took his degree from Cambridge University in 1915. During the World War he served as sergeant-instructor to a Signal-Service Depot and then went with the British Expeditionary Force to Salonica as a commissioned officer in the Signal Service. Returning from the war, he devoted himself to the study of psychology and wrote his first book,* An Introduction to the Psychology of Religion *in 1923. The next year he was put in charge of the Psychological Department at Glasgow University where he still teaches. His second book,* Control of the Mind, *appeared in 1928 and since then he has written other books in the same field as well as a short biography of Lady Julian, the mystic of Norwich.* How to Think Straight *is a completely revised and enlarged edition of his* Straight and Crooked Thinking *which was first published in the United States in 1932.*